Also by Thomas T. Noguchi, M.D.,
with Joseph DiMona
CORONER

CORONER AT LARGE

Thomas T. Noguchi, M.D.

with Joseph DiMona

Simon and Schuster   New York

Published by Simon and Schuster
A Division of Simon & Schuster, Inc.
Simon & Schuster Building
Rockefeller Center
1230 Avenue of the Americas
New York, New York 10020
SIMON AND SCHUSTER and colophon are registered trademarks
of Simon & Schuster, Inc.
Designed by Karolina Harris
Manufactured in the United States of America

10 9 8 7 6 5 4 3 2 1

Library of Congress Cataloging-in-Publication Data
Noguchi, Thomas T., date.
   Coroner at large.
   1. Medical jurisprudence—Case studies.
2. Forensic pathology—Case studies. 3. Trials
(Murder)   I. DiMona, Joseph. II. Title.
RA1053.N64   1985   614'.1   85-24975
ISBN 0-671-54462-4

To my brothers, Kazuo and Tatsuo, and their families, to the delegates of the World Association on Medical Law, and to my fellow Medical Examiners and the hard-working employees in the Los Angeles County Medical Examiner's Office

Contents

Contents 8

Preface

Did the urbane Claus von Bülow twice attempt to murder his rich socialite wife, Sunny, by the surreptitious injection of insulin? Did Jean Harris, the attractive middle-aged headmistress of an exclusive private school, murder her lover, Dr. Herman Tarnower, the "Scarsdale Diet Doctor," or was she really trying to commit suicide? Did Dr. Jeffrey MacDonald, the "All-American Boy," slaughter his pregnant wife and two young daughters, or were they massacred by hippie intruders? Did playboy Buddy Jacobsen kill a rival, Jack Tupper, for the love of the beautiful model Melanie Cain, or was he framed?

These were questions asked of me over and over again after the publication of my book *Coroner*. Americans everywhere were fascinated by these controversial cases, and wanted to know my opinions of them. To each questioner I responded that all of these cases had occurred outside my jurisdiction as Chief Medical Examiner of Los Angeles County, and I was not in possession of the detailed facts. But my interest was piqued, and when I began to look into these puzzling cases I quickly realized an amazing fact: all four actually pivoted on forensic evidence—and, chillingly, it was possible that such forensic evidence might not have been correctly understood by the juries. If so, innocent men and women had been convicted of crimes they did not commit.

Circumstantial evidence, and even the courtroom demeanor of the defendant (as in the Jean Harris trial), had also played a role in every case, but forensic science had provided the evidence that really convicted all of the defendants: an insulin encrusted hypodermic needle discovered in Claus von Bülow's "little black bag"; Jeff MacDonald's pajama top; the bullet wounds in Dr. Tarnower's body; the bullet shell found in a wastebasket in Buddy Jacobsen's apartment.

As I probed deeper into these cases, I became aware of the vital necessity for Americans to know more about forensic science, if justice is to be served in trials where lives are at stake. The science of forensic medicine, begun in a small corner of a police prefecture in France, then nurtured in London, Berlin and Tokyo, has lately begun to gain recognition in this country. But my own experience has shown me that our science is still baffling to many laymen. It should not be so, for our mission is simple. In forensic science we search for answers to unexplained deaths, not only in murders, but in suicides, accidents, drug overdoses, drownings, hangings, falls and a multiple variety of violent or abrupt endings to life. Our goal is to discover information that can be utilized in two ways: by the law in trials and other legal proceedings, and by medical men for the betterment of public health.

In this book, I have attempted to tell the full story of forensic science for the first time by showing it in action. To do so, I have undertaken the role of forensic detective, investigating in depth the four most famous and controversial cases in recent American history, and a fifth—the death of Roberto Calvi, "the Vatican Banker"—that occurred in England. I have also in-

cluded other mysteries and unexplained deaths in
Hollywood and in Nashville, Tennessee. And I have
delved into famous forensic puzzles of the past, both
in America and abroad. I have traveled thousands of
miles—from my home in California to Scarsdale, New
York, to London, England—to investigate these enduring mysteries, and I have been aided in my endeavor by the worldwide network of forensic
scientists who are both my colleagues and my friends.

And so I invite you to join me in my travels to ex-
plore the fascinating field of forensic science, and to
share with me the discovery and examination of telltale forensic clues. Because of them, justice was or—
perhaps—was not done. And you will see why.

THE UNANSWERED QUESTION: *The Claus von Bülow Case*

1

No judicial proceedings in recent history have aroused greater public curiosity than the two trials in which Claus von Bülow was accused of the attempted murder of his wife, Martha "Sunny" von Bülow. Press coverage was exhaustive, and both trials were broadcast in their entirety on television—an almost unprecedented occurrence. Viewers were able to follow the intricate legal maneuvers of the prosecution and the defense, listen to testimony and see revealing gestures and facial expressions as if they themselves were in the courtroom. Twice, Von Bülow was to be judged not only before a jury of twelve men and women, but before an audience of millions. And, in a twist that might strain the credulity of even the most jaded television viewers, his first trial resulted in conviction, the second in acquittal.

What more is there to be said about a real-life drama that has already inspired so much comment and speculation? My investigation of the case was centered around a key question. With her husband's innocence established, where does the blame reside for the tragic condition of Sunny von Bülow, still lying helpless in an irreversible coma?

2

Newport, Rhode Island, is perhaps America's preeminent domain of the rich. There, decades ago, the aristocrats of our society built sprawling mansions, extravagant imitations of the great houses of the European aristocrats they so much admired. Time and inflation have caused many of these mansions to be sold, turned into museums or simply shuttered up because even their rich owners could not afford their upkeep.

But a few of the great houses that line Cliff Walk are still open and in use. And among the most beautiful of them is Clarendon Court, the "summer place" of Sunny von Bülow and her husband, Claus. In fact, in 1950 the house was chosen as one of the settings for a movie about the tangled love affairs of a beautiful heiress, a movie called, appropriately enough, *High Society*.

Sunny von Bülow could have played that role. Her father, George Crawford, was a utilities magnate of immense wealth. He was also seventy-one years old when his only child was born. He died a few years later, and his young wife, Annie Laurie, and her mother, Mrs. Robert Wormack, also a very rich woman, raised the fatherless child. Otherwise, Sunny's childhood and adolescence were normal for those of her wealth and social background: private schools, chauffeur-driven limousines, "seasons" in New York,

Newport, Palm Beach and Europe. There the lovely young American heiress almost inevitably met a handsome but penniless Austrian prince, Alfie von Auersperg. And in 1957, almost as inevitably, she married him.

Two children were born of this marriage, but it did not last and Sunny again married a European, this time the mature, urbane Claus von Bülow, a Danish aristocrat whose pedigree, while distinguished, did not match that of her first husband, the Austrian prince. In fact, there were some who believed Claus von Bülow was a social climber determined to wed a rich woman. But others believed Sunny was the fortunate one of the two, because Von Bülow was so charming. Several years after their marriage, his charm would be evinced in a strange setting: outside a courtroom in Newport, Rhode Island, where Von Bülow was being tried for twice attempting to murder his rich wife.

The events that climaxed in the trial had occurred on a typical evening for the Von Bülows. That "typical" evening was not, as one might imagine, a great ball, a festive dinner, or a magnificent lawn party with white-coated servants carrying trays of champagne. Instead, the incredibly rich Von Bülows had a little family dinner at home, then stood in line at a local movie house to buy tickets. Two of Sunny's children, Alexander von Auersperg, by her first marriage, and Cosima von Bülow, whose father was Claus, ate dinner with their parents that night. The dinner was earlier than usual so that they would arrive at the Jane Pickens Theatre in Newport in time for the first showing of *9 to 5*, with Jane Fonda, Dolly Parton and Lily Tomlin.

Sunny complained of a headache at dinner but was

otherwise in good spirits. And instead of eating the main course, she asked the butler to bring her a large helping of vanilla ice cream with the special caramel sauce that the cook always kept in jars in the refrigerator for her.

At nine o'clock the four family members returned from the movie. Von Bülow went to his study to telephone an aide in New York on business. The other three adjourned to the library, Sunny excusing herself to go to the bathroom. She was back in only a few minutes, having changed into a dressing gown, and carried a glass containing a beverage that appeared to be ginger ale. She then chatted with her children for half an hour. At this point, Von Bülow came out of his study and asked his wife if she wanted anything. She said she would like a cup of chicken soup, if there was any left from dinner. Von Bülow left the room to get it.

While he was out of the room, Sunny suddenly looked weak and her voice started to grow so faint that Alexander had trouble hearing her. Von Bülow returned from the kitchen with the soup, which he placed before her, then went back to his study to resume his telephone calls to New York. But meanwhile Sunny became weaker and weaker. She got up, and seemed to stagger. Alexander rushed over, picked her up and half carried her to her bedroom. Then he returned to tell Von Bülow, who was still in his study on the telephone, that his mother was ill.

When Von Bülow arrived in the bedroom, Sunny was under the bedcovers. She asked her husband whom he had been speaking to on the phone, and he told her it was a business associate. While this conversation was going on, Alexander, according to his later testimony, searched the bathroom and the bedside tables looking for any drugs she might have taken. He said he found none. As he was about to leave, Sunny asked him to open the window. Apparently she liked to sleep in a cold room, with an electric blanket to keep her body warm. Alexander opened the window, then left his mother and stepfather, who were conversing normally.

When Von Bülow awoke at five-thirty the next morning, according to his later testimony, he found Sunny sleeping normally. He arose, let their dogs out of the bedroom, then showered and shaved. As was his habit, he took a brisk morning walk. And when he returned, he read the morning newspaper.

At 8 A.M. he passed through the bedroom to his study to resume his call to his Shearson–American Express co-worker Margaret Neilly, with whom he had been speaking the night before. They spent an hour discussing a financial report which they couldn't understand, finally discovering that an irrelevant page had been inserted by mistake, thus rendering the whole report indecipherable.

Von Bülow was furious. To clear his anger he decided to take another walk in the fresh air, far from financial reports and bungling accountants. When he returned, it was almost eleven o'clock and both Alexander and Cosima were having breakfast. Surprised to find that Sunny was not yet up, he went to the bedroom to check on his wife, and found that she wasn't in bed. Then he looked into the bathroom, and saw a terrible scene.

His wife lay sprawled across the pink marble floor, her head under the toilet. Water was running in the basin of the sink. She was breathing, but icy cold to the touch.

Von Bülow quickly summoned Alexander and telephoned for an ambulance.

3

When Sunny von Bülow arrived at the hospital, her body temperature was an astonishingly low 81.6 degrees, and her low pulse rate, highly constricted pupils and other symptoms showed that she was deeply comatose. Dr. Gerhard Meier, on duty that day, looked for needle marks but found none. He ordered routine blood tests and then went to speak to Von Bülow about his wife's medical history. Von Bülow said that she had taken only one Seconal. In the middle of this conversation, a nurse rushed in to say that Sunny had suffered cardiac arrest, and Dr. Meier went to her bedside to resuscitate her. When she was stabilized, he gave her the first of several glucose "pushes," a routine treatment for unconscious patients to determine if their illness involves low sugar in the blood.

Eventually it would be found that the repeated glucose pushes lowered the blood sugar instead of elevating it as it should have done, an indication that there was an excess of insulin, which "eats" sugar, in Sunny's blood. It was this finding that would later form the core of the case against Von Bülow, who was charged with attempting to murder his wife by the surreptitious injection of insulin. At the time, however, all the facts seemed to point to Von Bülow's innocence of any role in her illness.

First, he had had no *opportunity* to inject her. The family had been together all evening, until Claus went into his study. While he was there, Sunny, in the library with her children, became ill. It was a surprising feature of the case against Von Bülow that the prosecution admitted he had had no opportunity to inject his wife. Instead, it was hypothesized that he injected her with insulin later that night after she had become ill for other reasons.

Secondly, Von Bülow claimed he had promptly called for medical assistance upon finding his wife ill —and thereby saved her life. And thirdly, he had saved his wife's life once before, just a few weeks prior to this terrible event, by rushing her to a hospital when he found her unconscious from an aspirin overdose.

Why, Von Bülow would ask, would he save his wife's life and less than three weeks later attempt to kill her? He could have allowed her to expire from the aspirin overdose if he was, indeed, a murderer.

Nevertheless, the state pressed charges, and at his trial a web of circumstantial—and medical—evidence gradually wove around him.

To begin with, Dr. Gerhard Meier testified to the presence of insulin in Sunny's blood as revealed by the reaction to glucose pushes administered when she arrived at the hospital. But had it been naturally produced or was it artificial insulin that had been injected into her body? Because he was so busy saving the life of his patient and did not suspect murder, the doctor had not immediately ordered the C-peptide test which would have indicated whether the insulin was artificial or natural. That test could have settled the case right there: if the insulin was artificial, it had to have been injected; if natural, Von Bülow was innocent.

But the most stunning early revelation in the trial was that, almost exactly one year before, Sunny had been admitted to the hospital in a similar coma. That

time she had recovered, but the incident fueled suspicions in the mind of her maid, Maria Schrallhammer, and eventually in the minds of the two
Auersperg children, Ala and Alexander, for the maid
said that Von Bülow had delayed calling the doctor
the year before, even though she had pleaded with
him that his wife was ill. And on several occasions
thereafter, Maria would later testify, she saw a "little
black bag" among Von Bülow's possessions, filled
with drugs, hypodermic needles and, on two occasions, a bottle marked "insulin."

It was also revealed that after her first coma Sunny's
health seemed to deteriorate, and that in April 1980
she checked into a hospital for tests. There, when it
was discovered that her blood sugar was remarkably
low, she was diagnosed as suffering from "reactive
hypoglycemia," which is a temporary reaction to an
abundance of blood sugar in which excess insulin is
produced. But the insulin output is not enough to
cause a coma, as Dr. Richard Stock, Sunny's family
doctor in New York at the time of her checkup, testified at the trial. Instead, he told the court, he believed
the cause of her coma was "the surreptitious administration of insulin."

Oddly, another prosecution witness, Dr. Kermit
Pines, one of the specialists brought in by Dr. Stock
to examine Sunny at the time of that checkup, dis-
agreed with Stock's testimony. He said that when he
had asked Stock if there was any possibility that
Sunny was receiving insulin injections, Stock had
looked aghast at the idea and denied it.

All during that year, 1980, Sunny suffered spells of
wooziness, with slurred speech. Then, on December
1, she took an overdose of aspirin, and Von Bülow
saved her life. Three weeks later in Newport she

was found prostrate in the coma which she still endures.

After that coma occurred, the children, inspired by the suspicious maid, hired a private investigator, Richard Kuh, whose fee drew gasps from the court: almost $100,000. But Kuh earned his money. He journeyed to the Newport home with Alexander and a locksmith to search for "the little black bag." The locksmith wasn't needed, because the key to the closet in which the bag was found was in a drawer in Von Bülow's desk. There was no insulin bottle in the bag, but Kuh did discover a hypodermic needle that appeared to have been used, as well as various drugs. When tested, the drugs turned out to be Amobarbitol (a sleeping pill) and Valium (a tranquilizer). And when laboratory tests revealed the presence of insulin on the used needle, the evidence was turned over to Rhode Island police. It was later introduced at his trial, and the web of evidence tightened more strongly around Claus von Bülow.

The testimony of two distinguished medical experts, Dr. Harris Funkenstein and Dr. George Cahill, further strengthened the prosecution's case. There was no other explanation for Sunny's low blood sugar and the presence of insulin at the time of her coma, they testified, than that the insulin was exogenous (injected). According to these experts, there were only two causes of excessive *natural* insulin created in the body, one from insulin-producing tumors in the pancreas, and the other from a disorder of the liver caused by alcoholism. Neither of these two conditions, they said, had been found in Sunny von Bülow.

The medical experts were cross-examined on the fact that Sunny had been diagnosed as having reactive hypoglycemia that very year. In fact, at the time of her routine hospital checkup in mid-1980, she had an even lower blood sugar count than at the time of her second coma. Could the coma have been caused in some way by her natural hypoglycemia? Cahill replied, "I know of no case in my experience in which reactive hypoglycemia caused a coma."

In sum, the insulin had to have been injected; there was no other explanation for it. Together with the fact that the bag found in Von Bülow's closet contained a used hypodermic needle encrusted with the drug, the evidence was damning. But, the defense countered, what was the motive? Von Bülow had plenty of money. Just that year Sunny had given him a trust fund of two million dollars as an outright gift. This plus his other wealth gave him an income of $120,000 a year, which, Von Bülow said, might not seem much to the prosecutors, but was "plenty" to him.

To supply the missing motive, the prosecution summoned a reluctant witness, Von Bülow's lover, Alexandra Isles. Lovely, chic, youthful, she was a former soap opera actress. But no soap opera ever televised contained more drama than her testimony, climaxing with the fact that she had given Von Bülow an "ultimatum" to leave his wife the very month Sunny was stricken with her final coma.

So the jury had medical evidence pointing to Von Bülow's guilt—and now a motive. In vain the defense produced witnesses who testified that Sunny often injected *herself* with drugs; and argued, finally, that if Von Bülow had attempted to kill her twice, as alleged, why hadn't Sunny said so when she recovered from the first coma in 1979? Would a woman continue living with a man who had tried to murder her?

The jury was faced with a dilemma. The evidence against Von Bülow was purely circumstantial—as it always is in cases where there are no eyewitnesses to the crime. Yet the weight of the medical evidence was so great that on March 16, 1982, Claus von Bülow was found guilty of twice attempting to murder his wife and was sentenced to twenty years in prison.

4

Like many thousands of others, I was intrigued by the Von Bülow case, but perhaps not for the same reasons. In my own experience as a medical examiner, I have encountered cases where murders were committed by the surreptitious injection of insulin. In fact, such a murder had once been considered a "perfect crime," for while it was possible to detect the presence of excessive insulin in the body, there was no way to determine whether it was naturally produced or artificial—like the insulin used in the treatment of diabetes—and therefore injected. That is no longer the case. Forensic science is now able to detect the presence of artificial insulin. Thus it troubled me that if Claus von Bülow had attempted such a crime—not once but twice—he would not have been aware of that fact. And if he had used insulin and hypodermic needles in attempts to murder his wife, why would he not have destroyed such incriminating evidence?

I could not subscribe to the theory—put forth by some of Von Bülow's friends—that the insulin and the hypodermic needles were planted by his stepchildren, or perhaps even by the maid. I could not imagine for a moment that they would do such a monstrous thing for any reason. But I did have a theory that could

explain the used needle and the insulin. Sunny loved
sweets; she adored such delicacies as sugar-rich egg-
nogs and ice-cream sundaes with caramel sauce; and
she therefore worried constantly about her weight. I
believed she might have tried insulin as a means of
weight control, but when she was diagnosed as hypoglycemic she realized the danger of the practice, and
the insulin and the needles were left in the little black
bag, along with the other drugs that she apparently
used.

That, however, was pure conjecture. As a medical
man, I had an even stronger reason to believe that the
insulin found in the little black bag was not the cause
of Sunny's comas, whether she had been injected by
her husband or had injected herself—a reason that
was not mentioned by any of the medical experts at
the trial, perhaps because it didn't occur to them: *insulin had to be refrigerated.* New insulin developed
within the last two years does not need to be refrigerated, but the insulin in use at the time of Sunny's
comas would have had to be kept in a refrigerator or
it would very soon spoil.

William Wright, author of the book *The Von Bülow
Affair,* described the maid's reaction to the "discovery" of a bottle of insulin in the little black bag, which
fueled her suspicions. She said, "What for insulin?"
As a physician, I reversed the question to ask, "Why
insulin *in a bag* and not in a refrigerator?"

Thus, my theories about the Von Bülow case led me
in a circle. Experts at the trial testified that exogenous
insulin had caused Sunny's final coma. If they were
correct, that meant it had to have been injected. But if
Von Bülow used insulin to inject his wife, he would
have had to keep it refrigerated. But where? The maid
saw the bottle of insulin in the bag, but neither she

nor anyone else saw insulin in any of the refrigerators of the Von Bülow households. There appeared to be no solution to the mystery.

5

Free on bail set at one million dollars (which he was able to raise easily) but with his passport revoked, Claus von Bülow appealed the verdict of his trial. Upon review of certain irregularities in the collection and the presentation of evidence used against him, he was granted a new trial, and in the early months of 1985, approximately three years after his conviction, the stage was set in Providence, Rhode Island, for what promised to be little more than a rerun of the nation's most popular, real-life television soap opera. In theory, the facts of the case had not changed. The change was in the team Von Bülow had assembled for his defense, headed by Thomas Puccio, the brilliant attorney who had made his name as federal prosecutor in the Abscam trials.

In those same intervening years, my own career had taken a dramatic turn when I was fired from my post as Chief Medical Examiner of Los Angeles County. My appeal was unsuccessful and I joined Los Angeles County–University of Southern California Medical Center as a pathologist and teacher. There, in one of the great hospitals of the nation, I was privileged to work with a superb staff of specialists in almost every field of medicine. And there, quite by chance, I met a man whose medical experience shed an entirely new light upon the Von Bülow case.

As part of the medical center's continuing search for

excellence, a "grand round conference" is held each
week in the auditorium of the hospital. Leading specialists present medical cases of unusual interest for
discussion among the physicians present. And at one
such conference, Dr. Francis Buck, chief physician in
charge of anatomic pathology, presented the case of
Willie Statum, a woman diagnosed as hypoglycemic
who had died of excessive insulin. Later, he came to
my office to discuss it in greater detail. Dr. Buck did
not know of my interest in the Von Bülow case, but
what he told me offered a possible answer to the un-
resolved mystery of who or what had caused Sunny
von Bülow's comas.

Intrigued, I did further research of my own and
wrote a chapter on the Von Bülow case in preparation
for this book, although I knew it would be impossible
to complete while Von Bülow's retrial was still pending and his guilt or innocence had yet to be determined. But a few weeks before the second trial began,
my collaborator, Joseph DiMona, who lives in New
York, received a call from Herbert Fischer, a law partner of Thomas Puccio. It seemed that Puccio had
heard of my research and wanted to know what I had
uncovered.

Puccio and DiMona met in New York, where Di-
Mona found the trial attorney to be extremely busi-
nesslike—and extremely unlike most defense
counsels he had ever covered at trial. Puccio possessed no deep hypnotic voice, no flowing locks of
hair, no flamboyant charm to mesmerize a jury. Instead he evinced an incisive intelligence, and an apparent willingness to go to the ends of the earth to
find evidence to assist his client's cause. In this case,
he persuaded us to let him see the unfinished chapter
and, after reading it, flew immediately to California to
interview me on the facts I had found. There I intro-

duced him to Dr. Francis Buck, and we discussed a medical phenomenon that, I believed, might change the outcome of the new trial.

That phenomenon can best be described in the conversation I had with Dr. Buck about the Willie Statum case as I had recorded it earlier. "Mrs. Statum had had a number of proven episodes of hypoglycemia in the past," Buck told me. "When she was admitted to the hospital in 1980, she showed an astonishingly low blood sugar count. And when we administered glucose, her blood sugar count went down, instead of up. So we knew excessive insulin was in her blood.

"In this case," Buck continued, "there was no question of exogenous [injected] insulin. A poor black woman in her sixties, she told us on another occasion that she had never even heard of insulin. So we assumed that the hyperinsulin [excessive insulin] in her blood was caused by one or the other of the two classic causes: an insulin-secreting tumor in the pancreas or a liver diseased by alcoholism."

Dr. Buck performed the autopsy on Willie Statum. "Her liver was not diseased or damaged, so I examined the pancreas very closely—and no tumors were present.

"In other words," he continued, "here was a woman who died of excessive insulin, and there was neither of the two classic sources for that insulin—and no injection. Now, that was unusual but not unique at this hospital. In fact, I had studied a case which occurred a few years ago where a baby had died of hyperinsulin, again with neither of the classic natural causes and certainly no injection."

"In other words," I asked Dr. Buck, "you think there's another natural cause for excessive insulin that could result in death."

"I'm convinced of it, from my study of personal

cases and a review of the literature," Dr. Buck replied. "And I also believe I know what that other natural source is: islet cell hyperplasia."

As pathologists know, the pancreas serves two functions in the body's mechanism. The bulk of the organ is made up of exocrene glands, which produce enzymes to aid digestion. Scattered among these glands are nests of cells called islets of Langerhans, which produce insulin to control the level of blood sugar. Islet cell hyperplasia, to which Dr. Buck referred, is a condition in which these islet cells increase in number. ("Hyperplasia" means more growth.)

"I believe that in rare instances these islets start multiplying naturally," Dr. Buck said, "and thus produce excessive insulin which pours into the blood, and the patient goes into a coma."

I then told him of my interest in the Von Bülow case and described what I knew of the circumstances surrounding Sunny von Bülow's condition.

"To all appearances," Dr. Buck said, "Mrs. von Bülow's case is almost identical to Mrs. Statum's. Like Statum, she had previous hypoglycemic episodes, and like Statum she went into a coma and there was no source for the excessive insulin. No cancerous tumor, no diseased liver—and no exogenous source, if her husband did not inject her."

Could islet cell hyperplasia be the key to the mystery of the Von Bülow case—a hitherto unknown *natural* cause for Sunny von Bülow's comas? That was the question I asked in my unfinished chapter. And I concluded that it was perfectly possible that she lapsed into her final coma from the same natural causes that struck down patients in Los Angeles. If that was indeed the case, Claus von Bülow was innocent.

6

When the second trial of Claus von Bülow began, it was clear that the prosecution intended to follow the same strategy pursued in the first trial: relying on the circumstantial evidence of the maid, Maria Schrallhammer, and of Von Bülow's former lover, Alexandra Isles, but even more heavily on the medical evidence which, I believed, had been largely responsible for the original conviction. As for Puccio, his strategy was yet to be revealed. It was clear that he would have to shake the credibility of the circumstantial evidence where possible. But even more important, in my opinion, would be the necessity to cast doubt upon the prosecution's medical evidence by summoning medical experts of his own. Dr. Francis Buck was among those witnesses whom he might call to the stand.

As it happened, Puccio was able to score several important points in the cross-examination of prosecution witnesses, even before he began his case for the defense. When he was able to establish that Maria Schrallhammer had started saying that she discovered a bottle of insulin in the little black bag only *after* she heard about a laboratory report which said that insulin had been found in Sunny's blood, a shadow was cast over the credibility of her entire testimony.

And then, in an unexpected twist reminiscent of Perry Mason trials, one of the prosecution's own witnesses, Dr. Janis Gailitis, Sunny's personal physician in Newport, rebelled on the stand. The jury was hastily sent from the courtroom and Dr. Gailitis revealed that he was being prevented by the prosecution from delivering his true opinion. In fact, he said that as far back as the first trial he had told the prosecutors that insulin had nothing to do with the first coma.

It was Dr. Gailitis who had responded to Von Bülow's telephone call when the first coma occurred, and found Sunny unconscious in bed, and vomiting. Then she stopped breathing altogether. Gailitis said that he cleared the vomitus from her throat and began mouth-to-mouth resuscitation until her breathing restarted. Sunny's first coma, so dramatically described by the maid who said it inspired her suspicions of Von Bülow, turned out not to be connected to insulin at all, according to Dr. Gailitis. Instead, it was caused by hypoxia, the cutting off of oxygen to the brain, when her breathing had stopped.

When the jury filed back into the courtroom and heard this testimony from Sunny's own doctor, the prosecution seemed to be in real trouble. But then they played their ace, Alexandra Isles. After having left the country, apparently to avoid testifying, Isles returned at the last minute to stun the court, and the defense, by bringing up new evidence of a damning nature never revealed at the first trial.

At the first trial, Isles had hurt Von Bülow's case by claiming she gave him an ultimatum in the very month Sunny fell into her final coma. Now the defense apparently had evidence that no such "ultimatum" had been given, so it was never mentioned. But Isles now said that after the first coma Von Bülow had telephoned her to say he had "watched and watched" his wife suffer all day, but then finally "couldn't go through with it" and called the doctor.

Her testimony electrified the press, and newspapers the next day said that Isles had, in that one sentence, convicted Von Bülow. Lost in the uproar was Puccio's reminder to reporters that Isles had admitted in the same conversation that Von Bülow told her that Sunny had taken alcohol and sleeping pills, which caused her illness in the first place.

And then Puccio began his case, and reporters had another shock when they realized that Von Bülow's entire defense would consist only of the testimony of medical experts. It was a risky strategy, because medical testimony can be extremely complicated. But the eminent medical experts called by the defense managed to make their points clear.

Dr. Leo A. del Cortivo, chief toxicologist of Suffolk County, Long Island, said that the ashlike residue found on the "used" needle, believed to be insulin, meant that the needle had actually not been used at all. When a needle is injected and then withdrawn from the flesh, the needle is cleared of all residue by the clinging skin.

As to the laboratory tests which supposedly showed the presence of insulin on the needle, Dr. Arthur H. Rubenstein, chairman of the University of Chicago Medical Department and a world-renowned endocrinologist, said that the test on the needle-"washing was impossible to interpret because of deficiencies in the procedure." The result of the first tests on the needle-washing revealed more insulin than could be accurately measured. The laboratory, aware of this, conducted three more tests with three diluted solutions, and three different results were achieved. "The problem I have with these numbers," Dr. Rubenstein said, "is that when you correct for the dilution, as they did, the numbers are not the same."

"In other words, doctor," Puccio said, "this sample was not behaving the same way that insulin behaves, is that correct?"

Dr. Rubenstein replied, "That's correct."

As to the tests that allegedly showed high levels of insulin in Sunny von Bülow's blood, Dr. Rubenstein was equally skeptical. "I find it impossible to assess the validity of the testing," he said, because of the wildly disparate test results on the same sample. According to accepted procedure, duplicate tests should be run on each sample, and the values should be no more than 10 percent apart. In this case, the duplicate tests performed by a Boston laboratory on the sample revealed readings of 0.8 and 350. The laboratory then sent the sample to Bio-Science laboratory in California, which had more sophisticated testing equipment, but, unfortunately, not enough blood serum was left to perform the necessary duplicate tests. So only one test was made, and it showed a value of 216. "The discrepancies make the numbers totally meaningless," the endocrinologist testified.

In any event, these and other witnesses came to the stand to testify that both of Sunny's comas had been caused not by insulin, but by hypoxia: the first coma from vomiting which obstructed the air passages; the second from cardiac arrest induced by drugs and alcohol, and complicated by her fall and hypothermia, a lowering of her body temperature caused by lying on a cold bathroom floor.

When the defense abruptly rested its case after presenting only medical witnesses, and Claus von Bülow had not been placed on the stand to rebut Alexandra Isles' explosive testimony, most courtroom observers believed that Puccio had made a mistake. In effect, he was gambling on the jury's ability to understand and evaluate medical evidence over the human and often emotional testimony of the loyal maid, the loving children and the former lover.

I had no such doubts. I believed that Puccio had made the correct decision because, as far back as the first trial, I thought that the evidence used to convict Von Bülow was primarily medical. And after my discussion with Dr. Buck I also came to believe that Sunny von Bülow's comas resulted from natural causes.

Or perhaps the word should be "unnatural." From time to time during the second trial, medical experts testified that Sunny had a "chemical abnormality" in her endocrinological system, without ever speculating as to what that abnormality was. Dr. Buck was not called to the stand, obviously because Puccio was attempting to prove that hypoxia was the final cause of the two comas and there was no need to analyze or speculate on the origin of the chemical abnormality that may have contributed to it.

In spite of expert testimony questioning the validity of tests that showed the presence of excessive insulin in Sunny's blood, I believe that excessive insulin *was* in her blood, and that it was caused by the chemical abnormality, islet cell hyperplasia, which sends powerful surges of insulin into the blood much more profound and dangerous than the modest surges associated with reactive hypoglycemia. As we know from the Statum case in California, this condition by itself can lead to coma. In my view, in both of Sunny's comas, hypoxia was the culminating event, but they began with that abnormality in her system and, aided by drugs and hypothermia, ended in the final coma.

When Puccio interviewed my collaborator before the second trial, he was surprised by my information that insulin had to be refrigerated. "Just think," he said, "a whole trial was held with experts, then an appeal was filed with long opinions by more experts, and no one ever mentioned that insulin had to be refrigerated."

Puccio didn't mention it himself at the second trial,

perhaps because whether or not the insulin had been refrigerated was not germane to his defense, which attempted to prove that insulin had nothing whatsoever to do with Sunny Von Bülow's condition. I do not know if Dr. Buck's findings, and my own belief in Claus von Bülow's innocence, influenced the course of Puccio's strategy. But certainly he must have realized that since medical evidence had convicted Von Bülow in the first trial, it was necessary to call that same medical evidence into question to secure his acquittal.

His strategy worked. The jury apparently had little difficulty making up its mind. Claus von Bülow was innocent of the charge of twice attempting to murder his wife by the surreptitious injection of insulin. There was no medical evidence to prove it "beyond a reasonable doubt."

The Von Bülow case revolved around the human tragedy of a woman, Sunny von Bülow, who lies in an irreversible coma, her family still divided and torn, warring in the media. But in another sense it was a battle between forensic scientists of opposing points of view. And for me, it was a dramatic illustration that a jury of laymen *can* comprehend the complexities of medical evidence—and that medical evidence *must* be irrefutable to secure conviction.

FOR LOVE OF HY
The Jean Harris Case

1

In 1984 I heard surprising news. The bedroom of the house in which Dr. Herman Tarnower was killed in 1980 had been preserved by its new owners exactly as it was at the time of the tragedy, with furniture riddled by a bullet hole, a window broken by Jean Harris in a jealous rage, a chipped bathtub where she had banged the gun trying to remove its jammed shells, and a bullet gouge from a wild shot in the floor of the balcony outside the bedroom.

Jeffrey and Valerie Westheimer, who purchased the home shortly after Tarnower's death, had not allowed any journalists or investigators to inspect the room, despite repeated requests over the years. But the Westheimers had preserved the room intact because they believed passionately in Jean Harris's innocence and hoped that someday, if she is allowed another trial, the evidence still contained in the room may help free her.

For me, the existence of that room presented a rare opportunity—and a fantastic challenge. In 1984, through the kind intermediation of an acquaintance, the noted New York attorney Michael Russakow, who is a personal friend of the Westheimers, I was exclusively permitted to inspect Dr. Tarnower's bedroom and examine the forensic evidence it contained.

On the day of my visit, with Valerie Westheimer as my guide, I climbed a small spiral staircase that rose vertically from the garage through the living room to Dr. Tarnower's bedroom. Emerging from the staircase, the only means of ingress, I found myself in a corner of a room with a low, peaked roof. To my right were glass doors leading to a balcony overlooking the grounds of the estate. Facing me were twin beds backed by a headboard containing books. A bedside table and a lamp stood between the beds, in front of a shelf in the headboard which held a telephone and notepads. In the aisle between those two beds, many of the bloody events occurred the night that Tarnower met his death.

I found the bedroom to be oddly designed. The beds and other furniture, such as armchairs and a television set, were all situated in just one half of the space, the area facing the glass doors and the balcony. Behind the high headboard was nothing but empty floor space for about ten feet, reaching to the outer wall, which contained a window (with a pane broken by Jean Harris that fateful night), and three-foot-high cabinets along the floor, used for storage.

On both the left and the right of this room, situated slightly behind the headboard, were "his" and "hers" bathrooms. Tarnower's bed was on the left as I faced it from the staircase, and his bathroom was on that side. The other bathroom was for his female guests. This, then, was the room in which the tragedy had taken place, and Mrs. Westheimer told me that Jean Harris, during her visit at the time of her trial for the murder of her lover, had said that she still "loved" this house. "All of my best memories are here," she said. Then she went to the balcony door to gaze out at the large pond on the estate and murmured, "I want my ashes spread on that pond when I die."

I was familiar enough with the Jean Harris case to know what to look for in that bedroom, but both Mrs. Westheimer and I were in for a surprise. We were standing near the floor cabinets lining the outer wall on the far side of the room behind the beds, and Mrs. Westheimer told me that the cabinets were empty because Tarnower's sister had removed all of his personal effects years ago. She idly slid open a few doors just to show me that the cabinets were vacant, then said, "What's this?"

For the first time since she had moved into the house, she spotted, deep in the dark recess of a cabinet, two pieces of cardboard about three feet square. She reached in and brought them out—and we both stared at collages made by Jean Harris for her lover, the first one dated New Year's Day of 1979, and the second New Year's Day of 1980, only two months and ten days before Tarnower was killed. The collages had never been mentioned by Jean Harris at the trial and, hidden away in the cabinets, were probably unknown to anyone else connected to the case.

A chill went down my spine as I read the words on those happy, almost exuberant collages, especially the headline on the one prepared just a few months before Dr. Tarnower fell dead with bullets in his body fired by Jean Harris:

HOW YOU CAN USE LOVE TO LIVE LONGER.

2

Dr. Herman Tarnower's house, a modern, rambling structure set in a verdant lawn that sloped down to a picturesque pond, was completely dark at 10:30 P.M. on March 10, 1980, when a car pulled up and parked in the circular driveway in front. A minute later Jean Harris, headmistress of the fashionable Madeira School, emerged, dressed in a smartly tailored suit, and looked up at the darkened windows of Tarnower's bedroom. "Hy" had not waited up for her even though she had telephoned to say she was coming.

A few minutes later she climbed up the spiral staircase from the garage in the dark, passing the level that opened on the living room, then paused. She had forgotten the flowers she had brought along on the trip from Washington. Hy would be angry that she was waking him, but perhaps the flowers would help soften his irritation.

She went back down to her car and opened the door. The flowers had been tossed into her automobile by a student at Madeira School as a friendly gesture when Jean Harris was driving away from the campus, at the beginning of her trip. Now they lay on the passenger side of the front seat, in a colorful little bouquet. Beside them was her handbag, which she had also forgotten on her first trip upstairs. The handbag contained a Harrington and Richardson .32-caliber revolver with five live rounds in its chambers. Jean Harris had brought the weapon to Purchase, New York, to kill herself beside the beautiful pond she loved so much.

Earlier that day she had signed her will and left

suicide notes in her home addressed to close friends at Madeira. At fifty-six, she believed that both her professional and personal lives were over. A controversy about her expulsion of three students for smoking marijuana had led to flaring problems with the school's board of supervisors, and a feeling that she had failed as a headmistress. Worse, her lover and confidant for fourteen years, Dr. Tarnower, a prominent physician and author of the best-selling book *The Complete Scarsdale Medical Diet*, had let her know that he was abandoning her for a younger rival, Lynn Tryforos.

Determined to kill herself, Jean Harris felt she could not die without talking one last time, to the man who had been at the core of her life for so long. She picked up the flowers in one hand and her handbag in the other, and started back up the staircase.

According to Jean Harris's later testimony, this is what happened next:

Tarnower, when awakened, refused to talk to her, even though she implored him, "It's not really that late and I'm not going to stay very long." She went into "her" bathroom, the one on the right, and discovered "a greenish-blue satin negligee" belonging to Lynn Tryforos. "I took it off the hook and threw it on the floor. By this time I felt hurt and frustrated . . . I picked up a box of curlers and threw them . . . they . . . broke a window."

At that point, Hy Tarnower, not only awake but angry, got out of bed and slapped Harris. The slap, she said, calmed her down, and now "I simply wanted to get dying over with." She stood at the foot of the bed, "picked up my pocketbook and I felt the gun and I unzipped my bag and I took out the gun. . . . I raised it to my head and pulled the trigger at the instant that

Hy came at me and grabbed the gun and pushed my hand away from my head and pushed it down and I heard the gun explode. Hy jumped back and . . . held up his hand and it was bleeding and I could see the bullet hole in it and he said, 'Jesus Christ, look what you did.' "

Tarnower went to his bathroom on the left side of the room. Harris, more determined then ever to kill herself, dropped to her knees to retrieve the gun, which had fallen on the floor under a bed. But Tarnower, returning from the bathroom, took the gun away from her, then went to the phone at the head of the bed and pressed the buzzer to his housekeeper's quarters. At this point he was sitting on the side of his bed, Harris said. "I pulled myself up on his knees . . . and I was just about straight, and the gun was there . . . on his lap . . . I grabbed the gun and Hy dropped the phone and . . . grabbed my wrist and I pulled back and he let go and I went back on the other bed. . . . Hy lunged forward, as though he were going to tackle me, and his hands came around my waist and there was an instant when I felt the muzzle of the gun—and I had the gun in my hand and I pulled the trigger and it exploded . . . and my first thought was, 'My God, that didn't hurt at all.' "

Still clutching the gun, Harris pulled herself away from Tarnower and ran completely around the bed to get away from him. There she placed the gun to her temple and pulled the trigger.

Click!

The gun had malfunctioned. She held it away from her and pulled the trigger again. To her amazement, this time it fired, the bullet plowing into a cabinet in the headboard of the bed next to her. She placed the gun to her temple again and pulled the trigger. Click! Click! Click!

Sobbing, semihysterical, she ran to her bathroom to reload the gun with the extra bullets in her purse so that she could kill herself. But she couldn't pry loose the cartridge shells in the cylinder. Angrily she banged the gun against the tub, gouging chips in its side, and broke the weapon.

She returned to the bedroom, and saw Tarnower lying on the floor, bleeding. She picked up the phone to call for help, but heard nothing. She didn't know that the housekeeper had left the extension off the hook. "I said, 'Hy, it's broken. . . . ' I helped him onto the bed. He looked exhausted, but he didn't look dying."

Thinking the telephone was out of order, she left to go to a phone booth at the nearby Community Center to summon help, but by then the housekeeper, Suzanne van der Vreken, and her husband, Henri, had already reached the police. A police car approached and Harris led it to the house, and stepped out into the night to be greeted by Henri shouting to the police, "She's the one! She did it!"

3

Jean Harris was arrested for the murder of Herman Tarnower and on November 21, 1980, went on trial. The charge was murder in the second degree.

It was a case in which both sides apparently were certain of victory. The defense believed that Harris's story of an attempted suicide would be confirmed by the evidence. The prosecution scented victory because it felt that no jury would believe that Harris, while trying to commit suicide, would fire no fewer than three bullets into Tarnower's body.

According to the press, most courtroom observers—and most Americans—agreed with the prosecution, and simply didn't believe Harris's story.

During the trial seven forensic experts, including my friends Dr. Cyril Wecht, the former Chief Medical Examiner of Allegheny County, Pennsylvania, and a world-famed pathologist, and Professor Herbert MacDonell, one of the country's leading authorities on ballistic and bloodstain evidence, testified for the defense. Their forensic findings caused great difficulties for the prosecution. In fact, in what may be an unprecedented action in a homicide case, Deputy Medical Examiner Louis Roh, who performed the autopsy of Herman Tarnower, changed his interpretation of his original autopsy report in court.

The credibility of Harris versus the prosecution began with the question of whether or not there had been a struggle. Harris said that the shots that killed Tarnower were fired while they were battling over the gun as she attempted to shoot herself with it. The prosecution could not accept the concept of a struggle, because it would indicate that the shots might have been accidental, or even that Tarnower's own hands had misdirected the gun toward himself. Therefore the prosecution's scenario included no hint of a struggle for the weapon. In its story, the shooting was deliberate, and from a distance. In the vivid words of the prosecuting attorney: "She confronts the doctor. She gets the gun. She is in control now. She has power. . . . The doctor [is] seated on the bed. . . . The defendant [points her gun] and shoots it. . . . The bullet goes through Herman Tarnower's outstretched [right] hand and enters his chest. . . . "

According to the prosecution's scenario, Harris then deliberately shot Tarnower a second time, in the shoulder, as he lunged toward her. Falling back, he brushed the gun, causing her to fire a third bullet into a cabinet built into the headboard behind the bed. He recovered, went to the bathroom and when he returned pushed Harris onto the bed, causing her to fire another wild bullet through the balcony doors. Finally, as he tried to telephone the housekeeper, Harris deliberately shot him once again, this time the bullet striking his arm, and he collapsed.

In sum, in the prosecution's presentation of the case, the three fatal wounds occurred this way: Harris stood at the foot of the bed as Tarnower sat up and held out his hand, and she cold-bloodedly fired at him, the bullet going through his hand into his chest. Then he lunged at her, and she aimed and fired again, the bullet going down through his shoulder and into his lung. Finally, when he was on the phone, desperately seeking help, she deliberately shot him again, this time in the arm. The two "wild" shots occurred not in a struggle but when he brushed her gun accidentally, and again when he pushed her onto the bed.

One of the immediate problems with this recreation of events was that Tarnower's blood was found on the cylinder of the gun, and indeed had seeped deep inside it. The forensic experts for the defense argued that this could not have occurred during casual "brushings"—the only times which the prosecution admitted that Tarnower even touched the gun. However, this was just one instance, the defense said, which showed that Harris's version of events was true, and the prosecution's was not. And there were many more controversial clues—beginning with the first shot through the hand.

In his original autopsy report, Deputy Medical Examiner Louis Roh had stated that the hand injury was a "through-and-through" wound, in which the bullet "had not been recovered," and that *four* shots struck Tarnower's body. But only five shots had been fired, and two of them were wild. So Roh later said only three bullets struck the body. The bullet through the hand, which he had previously thought was not recovered, had actually entered Tarnower's chest, causing both wounds.

This new testimony was important because if Harris had fired through an outstretched hand into Tarnower's chest, she was a deliberate murderer. If instead the gun was fired during a struggle at the foot of the bed, and the bullet had lodged not in Tarnower's body but somewhere else in the room, it supported her story that she was trying to commit suicide.

The issue was Jean Harris's credibility—and so a war raged in court over that first shot.

The defense sent ballistics expert Herbert Mac-Donell to the scene of the crime with Jean Harris to reenact the shooting. There MacDonell discovered a hole in the glass balcony door, and a bullet gouge in the balcony floor outside. When he drew a string from the gouge through the bullet hole in the glass door, its trajectory led directly to the spot at the foot of the bed where Harris said she had fired the first shot in an attempt to kill herself.

When MacDonell testified about his on-the-scene inspection, the prosecution team battled back on two fronts: one, they claimed that the gouge on the balcony floor was not a bullet gouge at all, and, two, they had "proof" that the shot through the hand had not gone wild through the balcony door, but, instead, entered Tarnower's chest after traversing his hand.

Back to the stand came Dr. Roh with an addition to his autopsy report. He now stated he had discovered,

after the autopsy, that there was "palm tissue" inside
the chest wound, proving that the shot had gone
through Tarnower's hand into his chest. Also, he said,
the chest wound was cylindrical, not round, indicating that the bullet was "tumbling" when it struck the
chest, so it must have struck an intervening object.
And finally, no "soot," or particles, from the bullet had
been found around the chest wound, which proved
that the bullet had struck another object, "cleaning it
off," before it struck the chest.

Forensic scientists can tell the distance of a weapon
from the wound in this manner. Soot around a wound
indicates a shot up to three or four inches away. Beyond that distance, up to about three feet away, no
soot is found, but unburned metallic particles will
be seen around the skin surface of a wound, which
forensic scientists call the "tattooing effect." Longer-
distance shots leave no evidence of powder or particles on the skin surface.

To the witness stand came seven distinguished forensic scientists who rebutted Dr. Roh, sometimes angrily. The so-called palm tissue in the chest, Dr.
Wecht and others said, was not such tissue at all but
collagen, a microscopic cartilage element found
everywhere in the body. The bullet hole in the chest
was cylindrical, not round, not because the missile
had first gone through a hand, but simply because
Tarnower was bending foward at the time he was hit.
The lack of powder or "tattooing" around the chest
wound meant only that the gun was fired more than
three feet away.

Thus the angry courtroom battle over the first shot
raged on and, I believe, fundamentally altered the
outcome of the trial, for a reason neither side planned.
That shot was significant in indicating who—Harris or

the prosecution—was telling the truth. Apparently the jury believed the prosecution, but there was much more forensic evidence that might have altered that belief, and this evidence was mentioned barely or not at all at the trial because of the time expended quibbling about the hand injury. Almost ninety percent of the forensic experts' testimony revolved around that one shot.

In the ebb and flow of courtroom battles, confrontation tactics often dictate the course of the trial and, in doing so, may obscure the most important forensic evidence. I believe that is what happened in the Harris case.

Courtroom presentation of forensic evidence is a problem which we in the profession know we must somehow improve, and progress is being made. In the universities today, courses in such presentations are being taught, but we have still not solved the basic problem of presenting clear, narrative analyses that juries can understand, because the American judicial system is based on confrontation, not presentation.

The fact that important forensic evidence in Jean Harris's trial was either lost in the uproar over the first shot or not presented in a way that the jury could understand was particularly damaging in this case because, more than in most cases, its outcome then had to turn not on the evidence, but on the jury's *perception* of the defendant herself, as to whether or not she was telling the truth. Unfortunately for Harris, by all reports she was a disastrous witness for herself, appearing arrogant and snobbish on the stand. Worse, during her time in the witness chair the prosecution gained the right to read a long, bitter letter she had sent to Tarnower on the very day he died. The letter was full of rage against Lynn Tryforos, and seemed to provide a motive for the killing.

On February 25, 1981, Jean Harris was convicted of second-degree murder and sentenced to a minimum of fifteen years to life in prison. She is now in the Bedford Hills, New York, Correctional Facility.

4

Because of its forensic aspects, I was intrigued by the Jean Harris case and decided to investigate it for myself. I began by reading transcripts of the forensic testimony at the trial, plus the news reports in *The New York Times,* various magazine articles and two fine books by journalists about the trial: *Mrs. Harris,* by Diana Trilling, and *Very Much a Lady,* by Shana Alexander.

Later on, as my investigation progressed, I obtained copies of the original autopsy report, the hospital reports made by physicians attending Dr. Tarnower's body when it arrived, and all the laboratory records of the various forensic tests in the case made at the request of the police by the Department of Laboratories and Research, Forensic Science Laboratory, Valhalla, New York.

From these sources, I was surprised to discover major flaws in the prosecution's scenario of murder. Like most people who had followed the case from afar, I had believed Harris to be guilty. But now, studying the evidence as a forensic scientist, I made one discovery after another which bothered me. First and foremost, it seemed to me obvious from this evidence that a struggle for the gun had taken place— and yet the jury had accepted the prosecution's contention that no struggle had occurred and that Harris had shot Tarnower deliberately, and from a distance.

To begin with, I noted that all the bullet tracks in Tarnower's body were clustered in one area, as happens when two people are wrestling for control of a gun. Further, the bullet tracks in his body were all at different angles, also typical of a weapon involved in a struggle. Other evidence of a struggle was the bullet wound in Tarnower's arm. The prosecution said that this wound was inflicted when Tarnower was sitting on the bed, telephoning the housekeeper, and Harris fired down at him. But the autopsy report stated that the track of the bullet in the arm was *upward*. This upward angle could not have occurred if she was standing above him. Obversely, it would have occurred if Tarnower's body was above hers during a struggle.

Also, Jean Harris was left-handed. When she was physically examined after her arrest, *bruises* were found on the inside of her upper left arm, and such bruises on the gun arm almost always indicate to coroners that there was a battle for the weapon. In sum, a struggle definitely had occurred—just as Jean Harris had testified.

As for the famous first shot, the prosecution's contention that Harris had shot Tarnower through his outstretched hand was disproved, I believed, by the location of the hand wound. The bullet passed through the fleshy area of the skin between the thumb and the index finger. In a struggle this is one of the most common locations for a hand wound. The victim grasps the muzzle to push the gun away, it fires, and the bullet goes through that fleshy area of the semi-closed fist.

I believed that the prosecution's version of the outstretched hand (and therefore deliberate murder) was wrong for yet another reason. The bullet had passed through Tarnower's right hand, and from my experience I've learned that right-handed people (as Tarnower was) do not throw up their *right* arm to ward off danger. Instinctively they put up their *left* arm, reserving their stronger arm for further use.

But perhaps the most glaring flaw of all in the prosecution's case, in my opinion, concerned Tarnower's trip to the bathroom. According to Harris, Tarnower went to the bathroom after the first struggle for the gun, which began when she placed the gun at her temple and climaxed with the hand wound. The prosecution contended that Tarnower walked to the bathroom after being shot through the hand into the chest, and again down through the shoulder. The bullet in the chest cut a major vein to the heart and pierced the lung. The shot through the shoulder was even more devastating, traversing the body downward for seventeen inches, fracturing three ribs, rupturing the lung and the diaphragm, and tearing into the right kidney.

According to Deputy Medical Examiner Roh, those wounds meant that Tarnower went into "irretractible shock" within five to ten minutes, when death occurred. And yet, after sustaining these catastrophic wounds, with only five to ten minutes to live, Tarnower supposedly walked to the bathroom, examined his injuries, then returned to the bedroom, shoved Harris aside, and sat down to telephone the housekeeper.

I don't believe that the victim of such wounds could have crawled to the bathroom and back, let alone walked, while so near death.

In further corroboration of Harris's story was the presence of soot around two of Tarnower's wounds, which indicated that those shots had been fired at close range, not, as the prosecution claimed, from a distance. In sum, I concluded that Jean Harris's version of events that night, not the prosecution's, was probably the truth. But how to prove it?

From my preliminary examination of the forensic evidence, I had determined there were two major facts I must research that could prove to me, once and for all, whether or not Harris had told the truth:

1. The blood trail that Tarnower made *en route* to the bathroom. If Harris was telling the truth, and Tarnower had suffered only a hand wound after that first shot, the trail should be a thin line of blood drops from the hand. If, instead, as the prosecution alleged, he had been wounded in three places, massive blood should have been found on the carpet.

2. The gouge in the wooden floor of the balcony. If that was really a ricochet mark of a bullet, as Mac-Donell testified, and its trajectory though the hole in the glass door could be traced to the spot at the foot of the bed where Harris said she was standing during the first struggle for the gun, then again Harris was telling the truth.

The prosecution said that the tragic events of that night began with Harris deliberately firing into the chest of Tarnower. Harris said they began with Tarnower pushing the gun away from her temple as she tried to kill herself. Murder or attempted suicide? I was determined to find out.

5

Herbert MacDonell, a tall bearded man, is colorful in every sense of the word and an expert in two fields: ballistics and bloodstain evidence. He is the author of dozens of books and articles on analysis and testing, and he teaches courses in the subjects at Elmira College as well as at his own "Bloodstain Institute."

In the summer of 1984 I flew to Binghamton, New York, where MacDonell lives, to interview him about the Jean Harris case at which he had testified for the defense. He met me at the airport and drove me to his home on a lovely wooded street. Inside, his house appeared to be a conventional suburban home, until he took me down to the basement and I suddenly found myself in a very sophisticated forensic laboratory, equipped with modern devices of all kinds for MacDonell's use in his profession. After a tour of his laboratory, we sat at a little table in his kitchen, the sun pouring in through a window, and I asked him to tell me what he knew of the dark night of Tarnower's death.

He began by showing a Christmas card Jean Harris had sent him from prison: "Merry Christmas to all your students. If the case had gone to jury right after you testified I'd have walked out a free woman.—Jean Harris."

"The actual physical contributions I made to the defense were never written up," MacDonell said. "In fact, "20/20" [the ABC television show] did a whole program on the Jean Harris case and never mentioned any of the seven forensic scientists who testified she was telling the truth."

On the kitchen table, MacDonell had assembled several large files filled with photos and documents relating to the trial. "Was Jean Harris telling the truth?" he said. "I checked every step of her story, and in every instance I discovered that the scientific evidence supported her story—and disproved the prosecution's."

MacDonell found a picture in one of his files and

held it up to me. The picture showed a string, tracing the trajectory of a bullet from the gouge on the balcony through the hole in the glass door to a person holding the string waist-high at the foot of the bed. "For example, the first shot," he continued. "When Jean and I were at the house together, she was out of the room when I ran the string from the bullet gouge to the position at the foot of the bed, so I thought I'd test her when she got back. I said, 'Jean, exactly where were you when that first shot was fired?' She went to the precise spot at the foot of the bed where my line had reached, when I did the test earlier.

"But then I had a bigger surprise when I finally got hold of the official police photos of the crime scene. The police had dozens of photos the defense hadn't yet seen. I got them—and realized why they couldn't have been eager for the defense to see them. Look at this."

MacDonell selected a second picture which was almost identical to the first, only this time a police investigator was holding the string at the foot of the bed. "They did the same test before I even came along!" he said. "The police had to know that the angle of the bullet shot was just as Jean said. So what did they do? They started saying the ricochet mark on the balcony floor was not a bullet ricochet, even though one of their own investigators admitted it was a 'fresh gouge.' " He shook his head. "The prosecution *hated* that bullet gouge."

MacDonell then showed me a close-up picture of the gouge. "Look at that. Unless someone took a knife and deliberately carved a large chunk out of the wood, that has to be a ricochet mark, especially as there's a bullet hole in the glass door behind it. So we know that Jean is telling the truth about the first shot."

MacDonell continued his argument. "And what does Jean say next? She says Tarnower went to the bathroom to check his hand wound, then returned with a towel around it, grabbed the gun from her, and sat on the bed while he telephoned the house-keeper."

"Yes," I said. "Was there a blood trail on the carpet? That would show us whether he was wounded only in the hand—or had two other massive wounds as the prosecution said."

MacDonell looked through his pictures and came up with a police photo of the carpet at the time of the crime that I had not seen published. I sighed. The picture showed a single trail of blood droplets, as I had thought should be present if Harris was telling the truth. "But the blood trail isn't the only evidence," MacDonell said. "There was hydrolized blood on the mattress where Tarnower sat, after he returned from the bathroom."

Hydrolized blood is blood mixed with water. It indicated that Tarnower had washed his hand in the bathroom. "Furthermore, I examined the mattress for bloodstains," MacDonell continued. "The other side of the bed, nearer the bathroom, had a cloth-on-cloth bloodstain from the towel he tossed there. You see, it all fits with her story of the hand wound.

"And there's also a psychological factor which makes the prosecution scenario ridiculous," he said. "If Jean had stood in front of Tarnower, deliberately firing away to kill him, wouldn't he have run out of the room yelling, 'She's trying to murder me,' rather than walking to the bathroom and back?"

He shook his head. "Now we come to the climax, the struggle that Jean says took place on the bed, and the shots she fired. She says she remembers the sound of only one shot—and the jury, and everyone else, says, 'Oh yes? If there really was a struggle, you pulled the trigger *three* times!' "

MacDonell leaned over and said, almost confidentially, "But I conducted a ballistics test of my own in police headquarters—and it proved Jean was right when she said she didn't remember more than one shot."

He told me he had fired the gun on the police pistol range. "The police thought I was testing discharge distance. But what I was doing was firing each shell *twice* to see if Harris had told the truth.

"You see, her story was that after the struggle on the bed when Tarnower was shot, she ran around the bed, placed the gun to her temple to kill herself, pulled the trigger, and it clicked. The reason it clicked is that Jean had loaded only five bullets into the six chambers. One of the chambers was empty. If it hadn't been, she would have been dead when she pulled the trigger." He paused. "She then held the gun out to test it, and the fifth bullet fired into the headboard behind the bed. What did she do next? According to her, she kept pressing the trigger, each time hearing a click. Do you see now why I fired each shell twice on the police range?"

"Yes," I said. "To prove she *had* kept pulling the trigger and thereby prove she really didn't know she had fired all those shots before, just as she later told the jury."

"Right," MacDonell said. "You can tell when a shell has been struck twice. When a bullet is fired, the gases from the explosion cause the back of the shell to rise. But the *second* fall of the hammer flattens out the back of the shell in a distinctive manner. That's how I could tell Jean Harris kept squeezing the trigger, and therefore didn't know she had fired all those shots on the bed. It's scientific proof that she remembered only one shot. She thought there were still bullets in the gun!

"So from first to last her story checked out, scientifically, ballistically, psychologically, and every other way including logically," MacDonell said. "And there are other clues. Here's something no one brought out at the trial. It's only a small clue, but again it builds up her credibility." He showed me a picture of the back of Tarnower's pajama top. "Where's the bullet hole in the shoulder?" he asked. I looked at the picture and saw that the collar flap of the pajama top that covered the bullet hole in the shoulder revealed no hole of its own. "You won't find it because the flap was *up* when the bullet struck," MacDonell said. "And why was his collar flap up? Because he was involved in a *struggle*, as Jean said."

That evening MacDonell gave a slide presentation of the Jean Harris case for me and some of his friends, in which he explained many of the points he had made to me earlier. The next morning, as I was leaving, he made one final and very intriguing statement. "I know of a test Jean took," he said. "She passed it with flying colors. But it wasn't admissible in court."

Then he added, mysteriously, "There's a tape recording of that test in existence."

Was he talking about a lie detector test that Jean Harris had taken—and passed? MacDonell wouldn't tell me, but if that is what he meant, why the test is still secret mystified me.

6

A few months after my visit with MacDonell, I discovered that the Tarnower bedroom had been preserved, and I would be allowed to see it. There I knew I would be able to check in person the two items of forensic evidence which I had decided earlier would be litmus tests of Harris's honesty:

1. The trail of blood to the bathroom. Was it a thin trail from a hand wound? If it was, Harris's story would be confirmed. The police photo in Mac-Donell's possession showed that it was, but from long experience as a coroner I knew that pictures often lie, because of the camera angle or the lighting.

2. The gouge in the wooden floor of the balcony. I was concerned about it because in my opinion a bullet should not have ricocheted at all from such a floor but would have bored straight through the wood. If the gouge was not that of a bullet, then the prosecution, not Harris, was right.

When at last I found myself in the bedroom of Tarnower's former house, I went directly to the foot of the twin beds where Harris said she had stood when that famous first shot was fired. I turned to look through the glass doors that opened onto the balcony, and admired the splendid view. The pond, larger than I had imagined, and the willow trees were graceful ornaments to the estate. At my shoulder, Valerie Westheimer murmured, "That tree over there." She pointed to a tall willow. "Jean Harris said when she visited, 'That was Hy's favorite tree. I'm so glad you saved it.' She was so in love with that man."

But I was concentrating not on love but on a gouge in the balcony floor outside. I began to open the glass door to the balcony, but Mrs. Westheimer stopped me. "I'm afraid I'll have to ask you not to go out on the balcony."

"Why not?"

"It's dangerous. We're going to have to rebuild the balcony, because the wood is rotten."

Rotting wood! I crouched behind the glass door and looked at the gouge. That explained the mystery to me. I knew from experience that if a bullet strikes rotting wood it will not bore through cleanly, as it normally does. Instead the wood will break off in chunks—and cause just such a gouge as I was seeing. That meant MacDonell's test was right, and the prosecution was wrong about that first shot. It had been fired, as Harris claimed, when Tarnower stopped her from trying to commit suicide at the foot of the bed.

I next went toward Tarnower's bathroom to look for the trail of blood on the carpet. There was no carpet. It was gone: one important piece of evidence in the case that had not been preserved, I thought sadly. When I asked Mrs. Westheimer about it, she said she had removed the carpet because of the blood on it. "How much blood was on the carpet?" I said. "A pool?"

"Oh no," she said, "not much blood at all. Just a few drops."

Once again the evidence confirmed Harris's story.

I was also curious about the last shot and went to the far side of the bed, where Harris said she had fired it. According to her, she had stood at the bedside near the headboard after Tarnower was shot, placed the gun to her head to kill herself, and heard a click. Then she held the gun out to test it, pulled the trigger, and the gun fired, sending a bullet into the cabinet built into the headboard.

At the trial the prosecution said that the wild shot

into the cabinet had not occurred that way; instead it happened earlier when Tarnower "brushed" the gun as he passed Harris who was standing at the foot of the bed. But as I examined the cabinet, I saw something strange. There were two gouges, not one. One was in the front corner of the headboard, the other was in the back of the cabinet inside it, five inches to the side. The angle between the two marks showed precisely—and with no other explanation—that Harris had stood at the very spot she said she was standing when she fired the gun. The prosecution, according to the Westheimers, had not inspected the room, relying instead on the earlier police photos of the scene. So perhaps they were unaware of the two gouges in the headboard when they claimed the shot originated from the other side of the bed, and at its foot. But here was further evidence that Harris's story was true.

Examining the storage cabinets behind the headboard, Mrs. Westheimer and I then found the collages Jean Harris had made for her lover. And, my investigation complete, I left this house where one night, four years before, a fifty-six-year-old woman in love, and despair, had come bearing flowers, and a gun.

7

Dr. Robert E. Litman is co-director and chief psychiatrist of the famous Suicide Prevention Center in Los Angeles. I first worked with him on the Marilyn Monroe case in 1962, and I don't believe anyone in the world knows more about the psychology and circumstances of potential suicides than he. I was troubled by the fact that Jean Harris had not remembered firing three shots, so I asked Dr. Litman about the case. I told him that Harris remembered firing only one shot in the struggle on the bed. And that one shot, she believed, was fired when the muzzle was pointed at her own stomach. Was it possible that she couldn't remember the two other shots?

Dr. Litman said it was indeed possible. "Often in police cases involving gunfire," he told me, "the trained officer cannot remember the number of shots he fired in the incident. That's because of shock, and here there was a second factor. When Jean Harris pulled the trigger the first time, she expected the shot to be fatal to her. She was psychologically prepared for death, and when it didn't happen her mind ceased to function, and all she remembers is that first shot which should have brought her death."

Thus all of the pieces of the case seemed to fit together. Forensic evidence from the bullet wounds to the lone blood trail to the bullet gouges in the balcony and the headboard revealed that Jean Harris told the truth about the events of that night from beginning to end. MacDonell's test in the ballistics laboratory showed she really hadn't remembered firing all of those shots, and Dr. Litman's psychological experience agreed with him.

A struggle for the gun obviously did occur, and if it did, the killing of Dr. Herman Tarnower could have been accidental, as I believe it was. My research into the actual forensic facts has given me faith in Jean Harris's credibility. I believe she was at all times trying to commit suicide and Tarnower misdirected the gun in the struggle. Therefore, in my opinion, a grievous miscarriage of justice was done in that courtroom, and Jean Harris should not be serving fifteen years in prison for second-degree murder.

And she would not be if she and Tarnower had

heeded the unconscious warning for both of them that Jean Harris had written on her last New Year's collage to "Hy." Not only "HOW YOU CAN USE LOVE TO LIVE LONGER," but elsewhere on the collage:

LOVE—THE SECRET OF HEALTH,
HAPPINESS AND LONG LIFE.

THE OTHER SIDE OF FATAL VISION
The Jeffrey MacDonald Case

1

Jeffrey MacDonald was the son of whom many mothers and fathers might be proud: intelligent, ambitious, and the most popular boy in school. Reaching adulthood, he became a brilliant, hard-working doctor respected by his colleagues and revered by his patients; a patriot who chose for his obligatory military service the toughest division in the U.S. Army, the Green Berets; a father beloved of his wife, Colette, and their two daughters, Kimberly, 5, and Kristen, 2.

And yet this praiseworthy young man, on one dark night in February 1970, allegedly smashed the skull of his pregnant wife several times with a club, and stabbed her twenty-one times with an icepick; clubbed his daughter Kimberly with three blows, then stabbed her no fewer than ten times; and, finally, placed his little blond child, Kristen, across his lap, knifed her seventeen times, and drove an icepick into her tiny body fifteen times.

Could MacDonald have done this? Or was that

monstrous butchery executed, as MacDonald has always claimed, by a "hippie" cult with clubs and knives, one of whom scrawled a word in blood—"pig" —across the headboard of his bed?

I had seen that word, "pig," in blood less than a year before the MacDonald tragedy when, as Chief Medical Examiner of Los Angeles County, I investigated the scene of the gruesome murders at 10050 Cielo Drive in Beverly Hills, where the beautiful actress Sharon Tate and three of her friends had been murdered by the so-called Manson "family." Now, according to the first news reports from Fort Bragg, North Carolina, an almost identical cult murder had occurred only months later.

I was curious about the case because of its Manson connection—and even more so when later news reports stated that Army authorities now believed that MacDonald himself had murdered his family. The charge was that he had first killed his daughter Kimberly; then, inspired by an *Esquire* magazine article describing the Manson murders, he killed his wife and their other daughter, attempting to cover up his monstrous crime by *faking* a similar hippie-cult assault.

I thought that this charge, if true, would be easy enough to prove. Because of my coroner's investigation of the evidence at the Manson crime scene, I knew, perhaps better than anyone else, how difficult such faking would be. In my opinion, MacDonald would have needed a whole shopping list of evidentiary items on that night to create all the false forensic evidence which would indicate that intruders had been present. When he was acquitted of the charge, I assumed that he was indeed innocent of any crime. Forensic evidence found at the scene had substantiated his version of the events of that terrible night.

Yet nine years later he was tried and *convicted* for the brutal murders of his wife and children. And the proof against him was the *same* forensic evidence that had led to his earlier acquittal.

How was that possible, I wondered? Forensic evidence can often be misinterpreted or misunderstood. But can it lie? In the strange and haunting case of Jeffrey MacDonald, it seemed to me that forensic science itself was on trial.

2

On February 16, 1970, rain slanted steeply in the night outside the house in which Lieutenant John Milne, a helicopter pilot, sat working contentedly on a model airplane. Fort Bragg, North Carolina, the largest Army base in the United States, had been inundated with the downpour for hours. But near midnight it eased and Milne opened a window to vent the smell of the glue he was using.

A few minutes later, voices outside his house attracted his attention. Milne went to the back door, "looked out and three people were standing ten or fifteen feet from me, going up the sidewalk. These three individuals were wearing white sheets, and I specifically saw the center individual to be a girl and two males on either side, and they were all carrying candles."

When the three reached the end of his building, they turned left into a walkway that led almost directly to the side bedroom of the house at 544 Castle Drive in which Green Beret Captain Jeffrey Mac-Donald, his wife and two small children lived.

At 3:45 A.M., SP4 Kenneth Mica, Company A, 503rd

Military Police Battalion, was driving through the rain in his jeep toward 544 Castle Drive in response to a call of "trouble." At the intersection of Honeycutt Boulevard and North Lucas Street, Mica looked through the plastic side window of his jeep and saw a young woman standing on the corner. What was a woman doing at that intersection at that time of night? he wondered. He estimated her age to be in the twenties and noted that she was wearing a wide-brimmed hat, which looked "floppy."

Mica drove on, and when he arrived at the house at 544 Castle Drive he found three MP vehicles already there. Together with the other MPs, he made a futile attempt to gain entrance through the front door, which was locked. They went to the back door and found it open. They entered the house, passing through a utility room, then walked into the master bedroom—and a scene of madness.

A young woman in bloody pajamas was lying on her back on the floor, her head bloodied and crushed. A man, wearing only pajama bottoms, lay on his stomach on top of the woman's left shoulder. On the headboard of the bed, a word was scrawled in human blood: "pig." Both of the people on the floor appeared dead, but when Mica crouched beside them he saw that the man was still breathing. Mica turned him over and heard him gasp, "Check my kids. How are my kids?"

Mica ran down the hallway, turning his flashlight onto the beds of two children in their separate bedrooms. Blood all over. He switched on the lights in the room of the younger child, Kristen. A large stuffed animal with comic eyes stared incongruously at the face of the dead little girl from inches away. Mica checked and saw that her body was bloody from wounds. In the bedroom across the hall, the body of the older child, Kimberly, was in even worse condition. Her head had been crushed, in addition to the stab wounds inflicted on her body.

Mica, shaken, continued down the hallway of this house of horror to the living room. There he saw an overturned coffee table, with magazines strewn across the floor. Back in the master bedroom, Mica found that MacDonald had fainted, so he gave him mouth-to-mouth resuscitation. When MacDonald awakened, his teeth were chattering. Twice more he lost consciousness and Mica revived him. But in his waking moments, MacDonald told Mica through chattering teeth, "I can't breathe, I need a chest tube. . . . How are my kids? Check my wife. . . . I heard my kids crying. I tried to feel my wife's pulse and I couldn't find it. . . . They kept saying, 'Acid is groovy, kill the pigs.'"

Mica asked MacDonald how the murders had occurred. MacDonald answered that there were four intruders, one of them a blond female with a big floppy hat, bearing a candle, and three men, one of them black. "I think I hit them," MacDonald said. "I think I scratched them."

Later, in the hospital, MacDonald said that he had been sleeping on the living-room couch when he was awakened by screams from his wife and one of his daughters. Opening his eyes, he saw his assailants standing at the edge of the couch, and before he could get up they started hitting him. In the struggle, his pajama top had been ripped and pulled over his head, so that it ended up entangling his wrists. He used the pajama top to fend off an assailant who was trying to stab him, until another blow knocked him unconscious. When he awoke, he went to the master bedroom and found his wife horribly slaughtered. He placed his pajama top over her nude and bloody chest, then went to the children's rooms, where he found them both dead from bludgeoning and knife wounds. He attempted to give mouth-to-mouth resuscitation to all three victims, but it was hopeless. He called the MPs, then lay down and embraced his wife.

Fayetteville, North Carolina, the site of Fort Bragg, had a relatively large hippie community, numbering about two thousand. The next day, while police filtered through the area, questioning its residents, agents of the Army's Criminal Investigation Department visited the scene of the crime—and felt a slight uneasiness. A flower pot was standing straight up, but the flower it held was on its side. Why wasn't the flower pot on its side, also? The coffee table was on its side, too, but when the agents stood it up and knocked it over it didn't come to rest that way. Instead, being top-heavy, it rolled over on its top every time the agents pushed it. Had the table been *placed* on its side?

What made it more suspicious to them was that the flower pot and the table were the *only* signs of violence in a room in which a struggle had allegedly taken place between a man and four intruders. Was it possible that *no* struggle had occurred? Was it even more chillingly possible that the whole scene had been staged? If so, who did it? Was it the man who had miraculously survived with minor wounds while the rest of the family was slaughtered by multiple weapons?

Among the magazines that had been found scattered on the floor from the overturned coffee table, a copy of *Esquire* caught the attention of the CID agents. Its March 1970 cover announced, "EVIL LURKS IN CALIFORNIA," and its featured article described the sensational murders of Sharon Tate and others in Hollywood by members of the Charles Manson cult. Were the MacDonald murders a copy-cat crime commmitted by unknown assailants, or had someone tried to make it look that way?

The next day MacDonald's closest friend in the Green Berets, Lieutenant Ken Hanson, made the CID agents even more uneasy, revealing that MacDonald had not only read the article on Manson but had been fascinated by it. In a press conference called by the Army to provide information about the surviving victim, who was still hospitalized, Hanson said that two nights before the murders he had visited his friends the MacDonalds, and Jeff MacDonald had eagerly discussed the *Esquire* magazine article with him, at one point saying, "Isn't this wild?"

The CID's suspicions that MacDonald had staged the scene now intensified, but their attempts to collect other evidence were botched from the beginning. Dozens of MPs had tramped through the house on the night of the murders, tracking dirt and grass of their own into the rooms, smudging fingerprints and physically moving evidentiary items. Worse, the CID's fingerprint expert botched the collection of prints. Incredibly, the camera he used to photograph the prints had malfunctioned. When he returned to redo the photography, he discovered that moisture had crept under the cellophane tape he had used to cover the fingerprints, and most of them were ruined.

Not only that, but a bloody footprint found in Kimberly's room had been destroyed when a CID man attempted to saw the floorboards to remove it. And the pajama bottoms that MacDonald wore the night of the crime had been carelessly thrown away at the hospital where he had been taken.

Nevertheless, through all the errors, the Army had made some progress, or so it claimed. CID investigators had analyzed the family's blood and discovered that each family member had a different blood type: A, B, AB and O—"a million-to-one-shot," according to some reporters who commented on this finding. But pathologists know that the phenomenon is common when the parents have different blood types. Armed with blood-type information, the Army had analyzed the bloodstains in each room to establish MacDonald's movements that night.

Furthermore, investigators had found fibers from MacDonald's torn pajama top in each of the bedrooms —but none in the living room, where the garment was supposedly torn, indicating to them there had been no struggle in the living room, as MacDonald claimed. Utilizing both the bloodstain and the fiber evidence, the Army thus created a scenario for murder far different from MacDonald's.

MacDonald had fallen asleep on the living-room couch while watching television that night, according to the Army's reconstruction of the crime. Awakening, he went to his room and found that one of his children had wet the side of the bed. An argument with his wife ensued, escalating into a fight. In the words of the investigators, MacDonald "obtained a club" and beat his wife, becoming angrier until he lost "all control in a blind fantastic mindless rage." Kimberly came into her parents' room. MacDonald smashed her skull, either "by accident or on purpose," and then carried her lifeless body to her own bed.

According to investigators, MacDonald then regained his senses and, realizing he needed a cover story for the murder of Kimberly, decided to eliminate the witnesses and blame all the murders on hippies.

He clubbed and knifed the body of Kimberly. Meanwhile his wife had gone to Kristen's room to protect her. There MacDonald hit his wife again, then dragged her back into the master bedroom and stabbed her with both a knife and an icepick. He then returned to Kristen's room, knifed her seventeen times, and plunged an icepick into her fifteen times. Finally MacDonald stabbed himself to simulate an injury by an attacker, and telephoned for assistance.

The Army formally charged Captain Jeffrey Mac-Donald with murder.

Protesting his innocence, MacDonald hired a civilian attorney, Bernard Segal, to defend him. Even though the handsome young doctor seemed eminently sane to him, Segal cautiously ordered a psychiatrist to examine MacDonald. When the psychiatrist concluded that MacDonald was not only sane but was also of a personality unlikely to commit such murders, Segal accepted the case. And within days he notified the Army that, instead of waiting for a military court-martial of his client, he would challenge the prosecution at the Army investigatory hearing, which, under military law, precedes a trial.

The hearing was, in effect, a real trial lasting for four months, with witnesses examined and cross-examined on the stand under rules of evidence. Unlike the trial nine years later, it took place when the events were fresh in the memories of the witnesses, and all those witnesses were available to testify. Yet in both trials, MacDonald's guilt or innocence would rest largely on forensic evidence. Thus, in the defense of his client, Segal first showed how the investigation of the scene of the crime had been botched by the CID almost completely. Footprints and fingerprints had been destroyed, physical evidence had been tampered with—

any or all of which might have proved MacDonald's innocence. Then Segal dramatically presented "proof" that intruders had been in the house. Mac-Donald said that one of the intruders, a girl, had carried a candle, and Segal revealed that candle drippings had been found in the living room and in Kristen's bedroom. Furthermore, the wax did not match any of the candles found in MacDonald's home, so it must have come from outside. In addition, unidentified bloody fingerprints had been found in Colette's jewelry box, from which two rings were missing.

To fortify his case, Segal next produced witnesses who had seen intruders in the neighborhood that night. One witness testified that she and her husband lived about two hundred yards from the rear of the MacDonald residence, and that night she "heard the sound of running and scuffling outside [her] open bedroom window on the second floor. The voices were of teenagers, two male and one female, in the vicinity of Castle Drive."

Other witnesses testified that a neighbor had told them that she was awakened that night by the sound of a car running outside her house; that she looked out the window and saw a girl with long blond hair running from the direction of the MacDonald home, and that this girl got into a red or maroon convertible as it pulled away.

The neighbor herself, questioned later in the hearing, said it was true that she was awakened that night by the noise of a car but denied that she saw a girl with long blond hair outside. Her denial may or may not have been influenced by a frightening episode that had occurred the day after the murder, when two young men pointed a gun at her home from a car outside. She had immediately called the MPs and had worried about it ever since.

But the most dramatic testimony by far at the hearings was the identification of a hippie girl named Helena Stoeckley who, Segal believed, was one of the murderers. William Posey testified that he lived in the middle of the hippie community across the way from Helena Stoeckley. He said that Stoeckley normally wore a white hat and a long stringy blond wig. At approximately 4 A.M. the night of the murders, Posey had awakened to go to the bathroom. At that time he "heard a car next door whip in . . . real fast" up the driveway. Posey heard laughing and giggling, so he walked to his front door, where he saw Stoeckley get out of a Mach I Mustang. Judging from the sounds, he said, the car contained at least two males.

Approximately a week later, Posey said, Stoeckley told him she had been questioned by the police about her whereabouts on the morning of February 17 and had told them she could not remember where she had been because she was stoned on mescaline. She recalled only riding around that evening.

But Posey's most sensational testimony linked Stoeckley directly to MacDonald. On the day of the MacDonald family funeral services, Posey said, Stoeckley had worn a black dress, black shoes and a veil and had placed a funeral wreath on her door in mourning.

Finally, Segal presented a motive for hippies to murder MacDonald and his family. Captain James N. Williams, an operations and training officer at Fort Bragg's medical facility, testified that MacDonald was the group medical drug abuse counselor. He said that one of his enlisted men told him that "they believed their men were being turned in to CID for being on drugs" and that MacDonald had the reputation of being an informer.

In sum, MacDonald's defense presented evidence that there had been intruders inside his home and in the vicinity at the time of the crime, and that one of them may have been Helena Stoeckley. And there was a motive for the killings—revenge against an "informer." This, plus the testimony of independent psychiatrists who declared MacDonald sane and a man who did not have the psychological background to commit such a crime, all seemed to point to his innocence.

In contrast, the forensic evidence presented by the Army against MacDonald seemed inconclusive. The presiding officer who functioned as the judge dealt with it the following way in the official report:

The Army said that fibers from MacDonald's pajama top should have been found in the living room if there had been a struggle, and they were not. The officer noted, "It is unknown when the pajama top was torn. . . . With the garment wrapped around the accused's arms, the fibers . . . may have, in some manner, remained with the garment until it was opened up to be spread across the chest of Colette."

As for the bloodstains, which the prosecution used to prove its scenario of murder, the presiding officer commented: "Considering the amount of blood evident in the killings . . . it is entirely plausible to consider that some of it contaminated the clothing of the assailants and was subsequently transferred by them from room to room.

Worse for the prosecution, the two forensic items that had triggered the entire investigation of MacDonald turned out to be false alarms. The flower pot had been placed upright not by MacDonald staging a scene, but by an MP with a sense of tidiness. And the top-heavy coffee table that "always" rolled over on its top and never came to rest on its side was personally tested by the presiding officer with the following results: "On [the presiding officer's] visit to the Mac-Donald apartment [he] knocked over the coffee table in the living room. The table struck the adjacent chair and landed on its *edge*."

On October 13, 1970, the presiding officer issued his verdict:

> In the interest of military justice and discipline it is recommended that:
> 1. All charges and specifications against Captain Jeffrey R. MacDonald be dismissed because the matters set forth in all charges and/or specifications are not true. . . .
> 2. That appropriate civilian authorities be requested to investigate the alibi of Helena Stoeckley, Fayetteville, North Carolina, reference her activities and whereabouts during the early morning hours of 17 February 1970, based on evidence presented during the hearing.

Jeffrey MacDonald was a free man.

3

The Army hearing in North Carolina of the Mac-Donald case and the trial of Charles Manson and his "family" in Los Angeles were held at the same time, although the Manson trial took longer to finish, ending in December 1970. There was certainly no controversy when Manson and his cohorts were convicted—

nor was there controversy when MacDonald was declared not guilty. Justice had been served in both
cases. My own gut instinct that it would have been
too difficult for MacDonald to stage such a crime had
been vindicated in a hearing at which all the witnesses and all the evidence had been examined.

In fact, I had almost forgotten about the case until
five years later when I attended a medical seminar in
Los Angeles. A physician from Long Beach, California, a city on the southern border of Los Angeles,
sipped coffee with me during a break between lec-
tures. "You remember that Army captain, Jeff Mac-
Donald?" he asked. "The one who was charged with
murdering his family."

I nodded, and he said, "He's living in Long Beach
now."

"Is that true?"

"Yes," my friend said, "and he's one of the finest
physicians I've ever known. He's head of emergency
medicine at St. Mary's and he works ten to fourteen
hours a day. He's always willing to drop everything to
rush to the hospital when someone wants him. And
he cooperates on all kinds of physician committees
engaged in different projects, as well."

I said that was wonderful, and my colleague continued, "But here's the funny part. The organization
which loves him the most in Long Beach is the *police
department*. Here's a man who was tried for one of
the most gruesome crimes in history, and now in my
little town of Long Beach he's the special pet of the
police. They even give banquets to raise money for
him."

I was surprised by his last words, and asked him
why MacDonald needed money.

"For his legal costs. Didn't you know? Some fanatical relatives of MacDonald's wife have pressured the government into retrying the case."

"But that's double jeopardy, isn't it?"

"That's what MacDonald says. But the relatives say MacDonald was cleared at an investigative hearing, not a real trial, so double jeopardy doesn't apply."

My colleague, a stocky man with thinning hair and rimless glasses, stopped talking for a moment, then said quietly, almost to himself, "How could he have done it?"

"You think he *did* murder his family?"

"His wife's relatives think so. The Justice Department must think so, too, or they wouldn't have called for a grand-jury hearing. But I *know* him. I've met him socially and professionally many times. The man is not only a dedicated doctor but a completely nice guy who never raises his voice, let alone becomes violent. It's incredible to accuse him of butchering his wife and children in a wild rage. He's just not the type."

Driving home that night on the freeway, I ruminated on the controversy. What a strange case! MacDonald, by all accounts, was continuing his reputation as a solid citizen, beloved of colleagues, neighbors and even the Long Beach police.

And yet the Justice Department believed he was guilty of the fantastically horrible murders of his wife and children. I had worked with legal authorities long enough to know they didn't move unless they were *sure* of someone's guilt. They were inundated with too many crimes to waste time on borderline cases.

Had my gut instinct that Jeffrey MacDonald was innocent been wrong?

4

The heat was brutal in Raleigh, North Carolina, in August 1979. Jeffrey MacDonald, intense, sometimes irritable, always bitter, paced up and down one of the rooms in a college fraternity house which his defense team was using for offices. He couldn't believe this was happening, he told one of the team. He couldn't believe he was here on trial for his life again, nine years after he had been acquitted of the same crime. Then he stopped pacing and said he had heard that the prosecution was going to admit it could find no motive for the killings. How, he asked, could they prosecute a murder charge without even a motive? Why would he have killed his family without a motive?

But then a member of the defense team soothed him by saying that the forensic evidence that would be used against him was the same as in the first trial. And a judge had ruled in favor of him on that very evidence.

In essence that was true, and it remains one of the most fascinating aspects of the MacDonald case to forensic scientists, making it almost a classic in our field. In 1970 at the Army hearing, bloodstains and fiber evidence had proved inconclusive, but now the greatest forensic laboratory in the world, the FBI's, had entered the fray. Ever since 1975, when grand-jury proceedings in this long case had begun, FBI scientists, led by a chunky, muscular assistant supervisor, Paul Stombaugh, had been analyzing all the evidence found in the house, and conducting experiments to prove MacDonald guilty.

Stombaugh's testimony on this forensic evidence stunned the defense and, for the first time, turned the case around against MacDonald. Before his appearance on the stand, prosecution witnesses withered under the cross-examination of Bernard Segal, who again headed the defense and again brought out all the incredible sloppiness of the Army's investigation. But Stombaugh was FBI, one of the masters of the finest crime laboratory in the world. And, in soft tones, he annihilated MacDonald as he reported the results and analyses of his tests.

Example: Fibers from MacDonald's pajama top had been found in the children's rooms. This fact, discerned by the Army in 1970 but ignored in the prosecution, was important evidence against MacDonald. because he had said that when he found his wife dead he placed his pajama top on her chest, then went to the other bedrooms to check his children. If so, how had fibers from this pajama top that he had left in the master bedroom gotten into the other rooms? Obviously, he had torn the pajama top not in a struggle with intruders in the living room, where no fibers were found, but in a struggle with his wife. Then he had worn it as he went to his children's bedrooms to finish the slaughter. Only later had he taken the top off and placed it on Colette's body.

Example: A crumpled bedsheet and bedspread had been found in a corner of the master bedroom. The Army in 1970 had made nothing of this. But the FBI had examined the sheet and found that it contained the bloody imprint of Colette's neck, shoulder and pajama sleeve, as well as the cuff of MacDonald's pajama sleeve. This was evidence that supported the prosecution's murder scenario, Stombaugh said, because it showed that MacDonald had killed Colette in

Kristen's bedroom, then used the sheet and the bed-spread to carry his wife back to the master bedroom, again as part of his staging of a crime committed by intruders.

But it was Stombaugh's next testimony that rocked the court, a report on a creative forensic experiment that had taken weeks to perform. Stombaugh said that one of his technicians, Helen Green, had folded MacDonald's pajama top "as near as possible" to the way it had been found on Colette's body. When that was done, it was seen that the forty-eight puncture holes in the folded pajama top exactly matched the twenty-one wounds in Colette's chest. In other words, the pajama top had not been punctured in a struggle with intruders. Nor had MacDonald gently covered his wife with the top in grief after he found her dead. This new evidence proved that he had cold-bloodedly stabbed her through it twenty-one times.

Jurors hung on Stombaugh's every word and his de-scription of that test. In fact, Stombaugh created in-credible difficulty for the defense. In the military hearing in 1970, Segal had been able to concentrate on evidence indicating intruders: candle-wax drip-pings, unidentified fingerprints in the jewelry box, witnesses who saw a blond woman and other intrud-ers in the neighborhood of Castle Drive. But Stom-baugh's forensic test, together with his other forensic evidence, so clearly labeled MacDonald a liar, and therefore a murderer, that Segal had to focus all his efforts toward proving that the FBI's experiments and analyses were wrong.

5

Segal's team of forensic scientists was headed by the distinguished Dr. John Thornton, a professor at the University of California at Berkeley as well as author of dozens of articles on ballistics, bloodstains and other forensic fields. Before the trial began, a local newspaper had billed the future courtroom proceedings as a personal war between two forensic giants, Stombaugh, and Thornton. And so it was.

Thornton and his colleagues on the defense team were certain that Stombaugh's new forensic analysis of the evidence was totally invalid, but they lacked the manpower and resources of the magnificent FBI laboratory to prove it. None of them could afford to spend weeks patiently folding and refolding a pajama top, as an FBI technician had done. But Thornton, a youthful-looking, bearded man with a quiet demeanor, had managed to perform some vital experiments and make some important analyses of the evidence. For example, Thornton said that if MacDonald had struck Colette with a club, as alleged, tiny droplets of blood would have sprayed on his pajama sleeves in "aerosol" fashion. But no such blood spatter was found on MacDonald's pajama top, indicating he had not struck her. It *was* discovered, however, on the bedsheet next to Colette, so why not on MacDonald's pajamas?

And in reply to Stombaugh's forensically electrifying folded pajama top, with forty-eight holes going into twenty-one, Thornton detonated a bombshell of his own. He claimed that Stombaugh himself, years before, in preparation for a grand-jury hearing in 1975, had examined the holes in the pajama top and charted certain of them as "inside-out" or "outside-in"; that is, each puncture revealed whether the icepick had been thrust into the garment from the outside or from the inside. But when the top was folded in the new FBI experiment by Green, the results did not agree with Stombaugh's own findings; that is, when Green folded the garment to achieve her forty-eight holes aligned with twenty-one wounds, many of those holes contradicted the "directionality" of the thrusts. That meant the garment was folded wrong in her famous experiment and immediately cast doubt on its conclusions.

Stombaugh's forensic analysis, in my opinion, had been intelligent and remarkable—but I believe Thornton should have scored just as heavily with his rebuttal. However, testifying in open court under the cross-examination fire of a clever lawyer can be perilous. Thornton was in midstride in his testimony when he was overwhelmed by a lawyer's favorite stunt—a courtroom demonstration.

In my time I too have seen laboratory research turned into mockery by lawyers with a clever sense of theater. So it happened to Thornton when he was explaining an experiment which showed that if the pajama top had been jabbed by an icepick while in motion, the holes would be round. The prosecution contended that such holes would be jagged and that the round holes in MacDonald's pajama top had not been made in a struggle with intruders, but when he had stabbed his wife through it. To prove his point, the prosecutor, Brian Murtaugh, held up an identical pajama top and asked the judge whether he and his fellow prosecutor, James L. Blackburn, could perform a demonstration.

When permission was granted, Murtaugh wrapped the pajama top around both of his wrists, as Mac-Donald said it had been wrapped, then swung it wildly in front of him while Blackburn slashed at it with an icepick—and the jury stared wide-eyed. The demonstration ended with Murtaugh saying "Ouch!" as the icepick nicked his arm, and even Segal couldn't help joining in the fun of the moment. "Do you want a doctor?" he asked Murtaugh, and pointed to Mac-Donald.

Murtaugh then held the pajama top up for the jury to see. Needless to say, the holes were torn and jagged, not round, which indicated to the jury that MacDonald's tale of an intruder's thrusting at him in a fight was a lie. Thornton's experiment in his lab had shown just the opposite, and he insisted in vain that the courtroom demonstration was not valid because there were no scientific "controls." The prosecutors had *wanted* to produce ragged tears, so they had slashed away, rather than stabbed—but the damage had been done. Newspapers reported the next day that the jury was obviously impressed with the prosecutors' dramatic demonstration.

That night Thornton made notes for his next day's testimony: "A rational scientist does not conduct an experiment when there is no intrinsic means of testing or evaluating the data derived. There is a seductive appeal to *ad hoc* experimentation of the Murtaugh-Blackburn type—but science must ultimately be . . . judged in terms of process, not product."

"Seductive appeal," however, won the day in court.

There was to be one more dramatic development in the case. For days anticipation had been building after it was made known that Helena Stoeckley had been found, and would testify. Potential witnesses had told defense lawyers that she had confessed to the murders many times. But others said that she was a dope addict who made up stories. What would she say on the witness stand?

The courtroom was hushed as she spoke in a monotone in response to Segal's questions. Where was she on the night of the murders? She didn't remember. Was she inside MacDonald's house? She didn't remember. Had she and friends committed the murders? No. And because of her denials the judge refused to allow other witnesses to testify about her confessions, under the "hearsay evidence" rule.

Later, on many occasions, both to friends in private and on television in public, Stoeckley again confessed her guilt in the murders and even named another of the killers, a man named Greg Mitchell. She said she had been forced to testify otherwise at MacDonald's trial for fear of physical harm from her cohorts. It is interesting to note, in the light of her later confessions, that she did appear on the witness stand with a cast on her arm, an indication of violence never explained. And shortly after her appearance on television, both Stoeckley and Mitchell died, in different cities.

Stoeckley had been the defense team's last hope, because Stombaugh's recreation of the folded pajama top had obviously so impressed the jury. Their fears were confirmed during its deliberations when a request arrived from the jury to have the pajama top brought in for examination. Later they found that on the first ballot less than a majority of jurors had voted guilty. After examining the pajama top, together with photos of Stombaugh's folded-pajama-top recreation, they eventually voted unanimously to bring in a verdict of guilty. In effect, that one forensic test had convinced them.

Jeffrey MacDonald, the "All-American Boy," stared at the jury as if uncomprehending. Nine years before, he had been found innocent of murder at the Army hearing. Now on the same evidence, he was declared guilty.

A few days after the judge announced his sentence, it was a bitter Jeff MacDonald who spoke his last frustrated words to the judge before sentencing: "I don't believe the jury heard all the evidence."

What did he mean?

6

In October 1984, I went to Berkeley, California, to interview my forensic colleague Dr. John Thornton. Amiable, shy, dressed in casual clothes, Thornton greeted me in his modest basement office on the campus where he teaches forensic science. He sat down behind his desk and said firmly, in answer to my first questions, "MacDonald did not get a fair trial. In fact, the physical evidence in this crime points more to his innocence than guilt. But that fact never emerged at the trial. The only new evidence the FBI produced at the trial was the folded pajama top, which Stombaugh did—and I think even the FBI was suspicious of that. I remember taking a walk with one of Stombaugh's FBI superiors one day and he said, 'Either Stombaugh did the best forensic work I ever heard of or it's bull.' "

Then Thornton said to me, "Look at this chart." He handed me a chart of Stombaugh's 1975 findings on the directionality of the thrusts in the pajama top as compared to the way the holes were aligned in the refolding experiment. The chart showed that in 1975, at the time of the grand-jury hearing, Stombaugh's microscopic examination had been able to determine the directionality of thirteen holes in the pajama top. FBI technician Green's refolding experiment years later placed seven of those thirteen holes in direct opposition to the direction of the icepick that went through them.

"The pajama-top reconstruction was the single most devastating evidence against MacDonald," Thornton said. "But directionality meant it didn't happen that way."

He paused, leaning back in his chair, then said, "As a matter of fact, the whole case may be wrong."

"What do you mean?" I asked.

"The whole case may be wrong because it's based on the Army's bloodstain typing. The FBI built its scenario against MacDonald on the bloodstains identified by the Army's CID." Thornton leaned foward. "There's a person I know who was working at the Army Crime Lab in 1970, at the time of the murder, when those bloodstains were typed. He told me that in 1970 the FBI had looked at the Army's blood typing and found it was different from the FBI's own blood typing. To my knowledge, this was never disclosed. And if the Army was wrong, it changes the whole case against MacDonald. Remember, both the Army and the FBI in 1979 used the Army's bloodstain typing to 'prove' where MacDonald went and create their murder scenario."

"Do you mean the FBI covered up?"

"I don't know. But I'm satisfied in my own mind that the FBI knew about the variance at the time."

Then Thornton added, "Bloodstain typing is treacherous, anyway. I would be astonished if mistakes *weren't* made, with all those stains. Very probably there could be technical errors. But here a man's life was at stake."

I asked him if any other new information had come to him since the trial. "Well," he said, "there's a witness who will blow the fiber evidence out the window."

The prosecution had scored heavily on fiber evidence at the trial, pointing out that MacDonald said he left his pajama top on Colette's body before checking on the children. If so, how had pajama fibers gotten into both Kristen's and Kimberly's rooms?

"You remember MacDonald's pajama bottoms had been thrown away at the hospital?" Thornton said, with an air of excitement. "I've just learned recently that a hospital technician who was on duty the night of the murder is now ready to talk. He's told Brian O'Neill, MacDonald's new attorney, that MacDonald's pajama *bottoms* were ripped from crotch to knee. You understand the significance?"

I understood at once. If the fibers came from the pajama bottoms, then their presence in the children's rooms was innocently explained. MacDonald had visited all three bedrooms in those pants, after placing his pajama top on Colette just as he had said, and the fibers came from the pants.

And, suddenly, I saw the case against Jeffrey MacDonald in a new light. The prosecution hadn't proven an affirmative case of murder against him. Instead they had proved only that MacDonald "lied" in his story. But that proof rested on three foundations: bloodstain typing, fiber evidence and the directionality of the thrusts through the pajama top. And now all three were either suspect or subject to very different interpretations.

"Then you think MacDonald is innocent," I said.

Thornton paused before answering. "I don't know. The only thing I know for *sure* is that MacDonald didn't get a fair trial."

He stood up and moved toward another office. "Want to see a model of MacDonald's house?"

I followed him, and saw on the floor, a three-dimensional wooden model, about six feet long, of the MacDonald house, complete with miniature furniture. There was the living room in which MacDonald had or had not fought with intruders, the children's bedrooms where they perished, and the master bedroom where MacDonald was found, stabbed and incoherent, half lying on the body of Colette.

Using the model, Thornton and I discussed the movements of MacDonald that terrible night as they were reported by him and, contrarily, as they were alleged by the prosecution. Then he took me back to his office and began to assemble a pile of large file folders filled with documents, and manila envelopes containing hundreds of photos of every kind, ranging from the CID pictures of the crime scene on the night of the murders to personal photos of the defense team at work in Raleigh, including Segal, Thornton himself, the defendant Jeff MacDonald—and a smiling picture of Joe McGinniss, who had written the best-selling book about the case, *Fatal Vision*. Both the book and a television mini-series based upon it reflected the prosecution's view of the case and left little doubt about MacDonald's guilt.

Thornton said he was still a friend of McGinniss, despite the book. "We don't agree on the case, but I respect his motives. We correspond from time to

time." Then he added. "I also hear from Jeff Mac-
Donald."

"What kind of letters does he write?" I asked.

"The usual, I'm afraid. Filled with grievances. I
feel sorry for him, but I wrote him last time that I will
still help him to the best of my ability, but I can't keep
devoting so much time to it. I told him it's a *case*—not
a *cause*—for me."

I understood now why Thornton was piling up
mountains of original notes and documents, as well as
pictures, for me to take away. It was as if he were
exorcising the case by giving me his valuable original
material.

Back in my room, going over the material, I found a
notebook which contained an inventory of the objects
Thornton had found when he visited the MacDonald
house with his forensic team during the trial. The list
began with a reminder of the husband and wife's last
happy moments together, on the night of the murder,
sharing a drink. "Two liquor glasses in the drying rack
to the left of sink in kitchen."

Then these items found on the walls and a bulletin
board, speaking, as if in voices from the grave, of the
everyday life of this typical American family:

Coloring book picture—"I Love you Dad"—and heart
Instructions for expectant mothers. Womack Army
    Hospital
Kitten card
Note and drawing—"I Love You to Mom and Dad"
1970 calendar
Valentine heart
Valentine card
Fort Bragg Catholic Church parish mass schedule
Recipe for holiday bread
School calendar

Child's drawing—"Kim"
Easter card—"Dad—Love, Kim, Kristy"

The MacDonald tragedy remains an agonizing mystery. If MacDonald destroyed his own loving family, then on this one occasion an otherwise normal man behaved with the almost inconceivable rage and cunning of a psychotic. But if he too was a victim, then the real perpetrators of the crime have gone unpunished, and MacDonald is serving a life sentence in prison for a horrible crime he did not commit.

After further research and reflection about the case, I am now forced to echo the words of my colleague Dr. John Thornton. Is Jeffrey MacDonald innocent? I do not know. Did he receive a fair trial? No, if the blood typing was indeed wrong and the FBI recreation of the folded pajama top was not valid. And doubly no, if the FBI was aware of a discrepancy in blood typing.

In the MacDonald case, forensic science was indeed on trial. But in convicting MacDonald, did it lie? Again, I do not know. But in light of the controversies that still cloud the forensic evidence presented at his trial, I strongly recommend that further investigation be undertaken by legal authorities before Jeffrey MacDonald is forced to spend the rest of his life behind bars.

THE LOVE-TRIANGLE MURDER
The Buddy Jacobsen Case

1

The alleged "love-triangle" murder of John Tupper on August 7, 1978, by Howard "Buddy" Jacobsen over the affections of Melanie Cain, twenty-three, a stunningly beautiful young model, was, on its face, an open-and-shut case. Tupper had been shot, stabbed, and beaten to death. Jacobsen's apartment, on the same floor as Tupper's, contained evidence of violence, such as a shattered mirror and a bullet shell in the wastebasket which matched a bullet found in Tupper's body. Even more damning, Jacobsen was later spotted at a trash dump in the Bronx next to a crate in which Tupper's body was burning.

In sum, all the factors leading to a verdict of guilty were present: a motive (jealousy), forensic evidence, and the testimony of a key witness, Melanie Cain, who placed Jacobsen at the scene of the crime.

Despite the apparently overwhelming evidence against him, Buddy Jacobsen said he did not kill Tupper. In fact, Melanie was just "another girl" to him, one of dozens. Tupper, he said, was a narcotics dealer, and had been killed in an argument over drug money outside the apartment of Joe Margarite, a reputed drug dealer who lived on the same floor as Buddy. Then his body had been dumped into Buddy's apartment. Buddy, believing that he was being framed for a murder and panicky that a police investigation would ruin his model-agency business, did not call the police. Instead, he had his construction workers take the body to a Bronx dump, then went up there himself to check what they were doing. It *was* interesting that Margarite disappeared the day of the murder. But the press, the public and, eventually, the police preferred the love-triangle motive, as outlined emotionally by Melanie Cain.

Buddy Jacobsen, the shrewd, streetwise boy from Queens who had grown up to make it big in Manhattan, was arrested and charged with murder.

2

Buddy Jacobsen's life was shaped by his famous uncle, Hirsch Jacobs, who was one of the most skilled horse trainers in the history of thoroughbred racing. Early in life, Buddy went to work for his uncle, learning how to care for skittish thoroughbreds. Then he went on his own as a trainer. Lacking the capital needed to purchase thoroughbred foals of famous sires at auctions, he created a new plan: to buy promising horses at claiming races and develop them into winners. This he did so successfully that for three years, from 1963 to 1965, he saddled the most winners in the country.

Then, an underdog himself, Jacobsen championed the rights of stable hands to a pay raise—and led a strike against the major tracks. Thoroughbred racing in this country was, and is, controlled by members of an establishment elite. Furious at the ethnic young Jacobsen, an outsider who was stirring up so much trouble, they waged a battle against him and his strikers, and won. Jacobsen lost his license and was barred from training horses at all the important tracks.

But Jacobsen not only survived a blow that would have crushed other men, he prospered—and in two ways. Financially, he turned his attention to real estate, and soon owned an apartment house at 155 East Eighty-fourth Street and another large property nearby. Personally, he discovered the joys of lovely young women, moved to Manhattan from Queens, divorced his wife and began the life of a playboy.

As a landlord, Jacobsen instituted a novel policy: only beautiful young models and actresses, aged eighteen to twenty-two, would be allowed to rent apartments in the building. When Jacobsen opened a model agency of his own on the first floor, the final ingredient for amorous fun was in place.

But future tragedy arrived in the person of Melanie Cain, a lissome blonde, only eighteen years old, who was an immediate success in Manhattan's competitive modeling world. The two fell in love. Melanie moved into Buddy's apartment on the penthouse floor and, in the process, became the leading model, and the co-owner, of his agency.

By Melanie's own account, Buddy was far from faithful. Once she actually caught him in *flagrante delicto* in the apartment with another one of the beautiful models. Tiring of his infidelities, she turned her attention to the tall muscular John Tupper, a friend of

Jacobsen's from Queens, who described himself as a restaurateur. After his death, the FBI described him otherwise, as a "subject reportedly head of a group that smuggles cocaine into U.S. from South America."

The mutual attraction between Tupper and Melanie Cain blossomed on a romantic trip to the Bahamas, but upon returning they had a problem. Tupper's apartment was on the same floor of the building as Jacobsen's. They would be living in close proximity to the man she had just abandoned, and Jacobsen was angry. He wanted Melanie back.

Thus the stage was set for a love-triangle murder. But, bizarrely, another tragedy would intervene—and cast its shadow over the future Jacobsen case.

3

Cheryl Corey and Scott Shephard were in love. Cheryl was a young model at the Elite model agency, owned jointly by Buddy Jacobsen and Melanie Cain. She also lived on the fourth floor of the apartment house at 155 East Eighty-fourth Street owned by Buddy, where Melanie was now residing in the apartment of her new boyfriend, John Tupper.

On the night of August 5, 1978, the two young lovers were on a seventeenth-floor balcony of an apartment house on East Eighty-fifth Street, perhaps embracing, perhaps just leaning against the railing of the terrace. Perhaps, also, they were pushed. No one knows for certain, because the railing collapsed, and the two youngsters fell through the air, clinging to each other. Their bodies plummeted through the back roof of a supermarket before striking the ground.

According to Jacobsen's later recollection, news of the tragedy to a tenant struck him like a thunderbolt when he heard about it the next morning. He knew that the police would soon be making inquiries, and the last thing he wanted for 155 East Eighty-fourth Street was police attention. The reason? Too many of his male tenants had underworld connections, from Tupper to Joe Margarite.

Knowing that Melanie might soon be questioned by the police because she was co-owner of the model agency which employed Cheryl, he went around the corner and down the hall to her apartment. Melanie told the rest of the story in court, at Jacobsen's trial for murder, which began on January 30, 1980.

The prosecution faced a problem at the trial. Even though the forensic evidence in Jacobsen's apartment was damning, the "drug angle" constantly kept intruding. Tupper *had* been fingered by the FBI as a narcotics smuggler; Joe Margarite *had* disappeared; and, worse, there were bullet holes found in Margarite's apartment, outside of which Jacobsen claimed the killing had taken place. So Melanie Cain's testimony would be crucial to the prosecution—both in establishing a motive and in showing Jacobsen's movements on the morning Tupper was murdered.

Melanie delivered handsomely. As to motive, she told of harrowing face-to-face confrontations and emotional telephone calls with Jacobsen, who was determined to win her back from Tupper and even offered a bachelor's last sacrifice, marriage. Yes, she said, he was jealous of Tupper.

But her account of the events of the critical morning was even more damaging to Buddy because:

1. It placed him in his apartment at the time of the murder. (Jacobsen's alibi was that he was out of the

apartment house completely at that time, checking the construction work on the building at his other lot.)

2. It revealed that his apartment was a shambles at the time she returned to it, shortly after Tupper was murdered.

3. It showed that Jacobsen attempted to cover up the crime.

This was Melanie's dramatic account of that eventful morning. She awoke just before 9 A.M. on that Sunday. Tupper was still asleep, so, after enjoying a cup of tea, she prepared to shower, and found there was no hot water. She left 7C, where she and Tupper lived, and went around the corner to 7D, where she and Jacobsen *used* to live, and banged on the door. Jacobsen listened to her complaint, checked his own water, then checked an apartment neighboring 7C, leased by a blond stockbroker, Leslie Hammond, who was away for the weekend. Hammond's water, like his, was hot. "Wait awhile," he told her. "The hot water will come on soon."

But, according to Melanie's story, it didn't, so she dressed in a gray-blue man's shirt, white painter's pants and Frye boots, and at 9:45 went back to Jacobsen's apartment to complain again. This time he asked her where she was going, and she said she had an appointment with a real-estate agent to sign a lease for a new apartment for her and Jack Tupper.

A few minutes later, Melanie told the court, Jacobsen knocked on her door to tell her that Cheryl Corey had been killed the night before. Melanie said she thought he was joking and slammed the door in his face, but later reconsidered and went to his door *again*. There Jacobsen told her that Cheryl Corey's two roommates on the fourth floor had telephoned him to say the police had informed them of Cheryl's fall from the balcony. Melanie said she would stop in at the police precinct house after signing the lease and find out more details of the death. She then testified that she reminded Jacobsen that the police would be questioning him because he had been out with Cheryl just two nights before.

On her way out of the building, Melanie visited Cheryl's roommates, who said they would go to the precinct house and find out everything, then went to the real-estate agent's, where she signed the lease for her and Tupper's new apartment. She said she then telephoned Jacobsen from an outdoor booth.

Why did she telephone her ex-lover whom she had been seeing all morning? Why couldn't she wait until she returned to the apartment house? Melanie claimed the real-estate agent had told her of a radio newscast which said that the Cheryl Corey tragedy was an accident, not a murder. Showing unexpected concern for the man who allegedly had been frightening her, she said she called him right away because she knew he would be worried.

Defense attorneys were suspicious of that call, because it was too convenient for the prosecution. It placed Jacobsen in his apartment at the time of the murder. Not only that, Melanie claimed Jacobsen's voice was short of breath, panicky and high-pitched. She told him she wanted to talk about what happened to Cheryl but he barked, "I can't talk to you, I'm on the other line," and hung up.

Arriving back at the apartment house approximately an hour and a half after she had left it, Melanie, for some reason, didn't go to her own apartment to tell her new lover about the lease and talk about their new apartment. Instead she banged on Jacobsen's door *again*. No one responded, but, she claimed, she heard whispering and clanging noises inside.

Later, after talking again to Cheryl Corey's roommates about the accident, she returned to the seventh floor—and found Jacobsen on his knees in the hallway, cleaning up the rug, which was now splotched with white paint. Jacobsen stood up and walked into his living room, and she followed him in. There she saw a shattered mirror, cushions from the couch strewn on the floor, and a fire in the fireplace—in August—and noticed that a rug was missing.

Apparently unconcerned about these obvious signs of violence, she returned to her own apartment, and found that Tupper was missing. Still unconcerned, it would appear, she dozed for almost two hours before setting out to look for her new lover. After checking around the neighborhood, she returned once again to Jacobsen's apartment and banged on the door. This time she heard not whispers but the sound of a floor sander, and no one responded to her knocking.

Later, back in her apartment, she heard noises. She looked through Jacobsen's peephole and saw Jacobsen engaged in activities the police would later term a "cover-up." Jacobsen and his son, Douglas, were cutting up the paint-splotched rug into fragments and stuffing them into plastic garbage bags. She also saw Jacobsen enter Margarite's apartment and emerge with paper towels.

The significance of the paint-splotched rug was obvious, according to the prosecution. The paint covered bloodstains, and Melanie had seen Jacobsen attempting to destroy the evidence.

The defense attorneys were vastly suspicious of Melanie's story, and in cross-examination they attacked it on many levels:

1. The sheer profusion of her alleged visits, and calls, to Jacobsen's apartment, many of them so convenient for the prosecution, was bizarre.

2. The telephone call to Jacobsen from an outdoor booth. What was so urgent? A *radio news report?* Had she really made the call, or had she said she made it to place Jacobsen at the scene at a time that he said he was not there? The defense pointed out that in a preliminary court proceeding over a legal motion, Melanie had not mentioned the "radio report." Instead, according to the transcript:

Q. Did you talk to Mr. Jacobsen while you were down there [at the real-estate agency]?
A. Yes, I did. I called him at a phone booth. To inform him about a previous death of a model that was in our agency who had fallen off a terrace building that night.

The defense pointed out that Jacobsen already knew about the death; in fact, he had informed Melanie about it, in person, before she left the house.

3. Her visit to Jacobsen's apartment immediately upon returning to the building also inspired suspicion. The defense attorney said, "You had just signed a fifteen-hundred-dollar-a-month lease for a new apartment for both of you, and instead of going to Tupper's apartment to tell him, you went to Jacobsen's . . . I'll tell you why you didn't go to Tupper's apartment. Because you knew Tupper wasn't there!" This implication was based on Jacobsen's apparent belief that Melanie knew more than she was saying about Tupper's murder.

4. Melanie's subsequent visit to Jacobsen's apartment, when she saw the apartment a shambles. The defense said Jacobsen's allowing her to walk right into the apartment, where he had supposedly just murdered her lover, was a strange action indeed. But, again, it was so useful to the prosecution.

Nevertheless, as Melanie left the witness stand, most courtroom observers believed she had survived intact, if slightly battered. After all, the forensic evidence in Jacobsen's apartment supported her story of violence there.

The defense had a different story to tell. It began its counterattack on the entire prosecution case with forensic evidence of its own, stating that blood had been found on a table in Joe Margarite's kitchen, a bullet hole in his closet, and two other suspicious holes in his bedroom window, all of which indicated that the shooting had begun in Margarite's apartment, and culminated in the hall outside when Tupper attempted to flee.

I was part of the prosecution's counterattack.

4

In January 1980, I received a telephone call from one of Jacobsen's attorneys, who asked me if I would analyze the blood found in Joe Margarite's apartment. Also, he told me, the police had found what they believed to be one of the murder weapons, a sledgehammer discovered in the trunk of a car belonging to one of Jacobsen's construction workers, Sal Prainito. (The gun and knife also used in the brutal slaying had never been found.) He wanted my opinion as to whether that hammer had been a murder weapon.

Medical examiners are officers of the county or other legal components of the state, and rarely receive an opportunity to testify for the defense in a murder trial. Instead, we're most often called upon to assist the prosecution with analyses of evidence. I told Jacobsen's attorney I would be pleased to give testimony at the trial, but that it would, of course, be impartial—and this proved more prophetic than I had expected.

Needless to say, if blood of Tupper's type had been found in Margarite's apartment, it would be crucial evidence in favor of Jacobsen's version of events. But the analysis of the blood done by my toxicological experts (for which Los Angeles County was reimbursed by Jacobsen's attorneys) showed that the bloodstains discovered in Margarite's apartment were not of the blood type Jacobsen hoped to find—that of Jack Tupper. Instead we analyzed it as Type O, while Tupper's was Type A.

Nevertheless, somewhat to my puzzlement, I was asked to testify at the trial, and a month later Buddy Jacobsen, a lean, smallish man with a mustache, a quick smile, and an attractive young lady on his arm, met me at the airport in New York. As he drove me into the city, Jacobsen talked pleasantly and seemed neither bitter nor tense. He struck me as very personable.

In court, because my bloodstain analysis had not produced the desired results, I found myself in a rather peculiar position. Very soon after beginning my testimony, I realized the defense attorney wanted me to say that the blood testing I had done for him was, in fact, not valid because it was not one hundred percent accurate.

It was easy for me to testify to that because all pathologists know that blood typing *is* treacherous.

The three steps in analyzing blood are: (1) Is the stain blood? (2) Is it human blood? (3) What type is it?

Until very recently the benzidine test was used to discover whether a red or brownish stain is blood. To test a dried stain in the laboratory, we take a sharp instrument and peel off a crust. This crust is dissolved in a saline solution, then applied to a Q-tip. Blood contains hemoglobin. ("Hem" is an organic substance containing iron, and "globin" is a protein.) When hemoglobin contacts benzidine it turns blue, and we know the stain is blood. Recently, however, benzidine has been declared carcinogenic, so we now use phenolphthalein, which is less sensitive, to determine whether or not the stain is blood.

We next discover whether the blood is *human* by a precipitation test. Rabbits injected with human blood, which is foreign to them, develop antibodies. We take the serum containing the antibodies and pour it into a test tube on top of the suspected human blood dissolved in distilled water. If it is human blood, a faint white zone appears between the blood solution and the rabbit serum.

Finally, we obtain the *blood type* in this way: We place the blood in two tiny wells of a tray. Then we take serum from a rabbit which has been injected with human blood A, and serum from a second rabbit injected with human blood B. We add Serum A to the blood in one well, and B to the blood in the other well to obtain the following results:

If the blood in the first well agglutinates (clots) and the blood in the second does not, we know the blood is Type A.

If the blood agglutinating is that in the second well, we know it is Type B.

If *both* agglutinate, it is Type AB. And if neither agglutinates, it is Type O.

This sounds simple and clear, so why have I repeatedly said that blood typing is "treacherous"? First of all, because the benzidine and similar tests used to discover whether a stain is blood can give false reactions. In response to the defense attorney's questions, I testified that there were a number of food and chemical substances, including citrus fruits and, of course, meats which contain animal blood, that can result in what we call a false-positive reaction. I also testified that bacterial contamination and the presence of body fluids like saliva or even sweat can confuse the determination of blood types. In effect, I was forced to impeach myself as an expert witness, as Jacobsen's attorney sought to prove that no one could be sure that the bloodstains found in Margarite's apartment were *not* of Tupper's type.

But I had better news, as far as Jacobsen's defense was concerned, about the sledgehammer. From examining the description of the two blows to Tupper's head contained in the autopsy report, I believed that the sledgehammer had not been used to kill Tupper. On direct examination I testified that the hammer was too heavy to have caused the injuries to the skull as described in the autopsy report. I pointed out that the sides of the skull where the injuries had occurred are thin, and would have been crushed. They hadn't been. And to demonstrate my point I picked up the weapon to show how heavy it was. A massive instrument like this, I said, would have caused not only deeper holes but other fracturing of the skull, called eggshell fractures.

The next day on cross-examination I faced a husky prosecuting attorney, William Hrabsky. His voice dripped with sarcasm as he said:

Q. Now, when you said heavy weapon, you were saying this is a heavy weapon to you, is that correct, Doctor?
A. Yes.

Q. And, you don't work on construction, do you, Doctor Noguchi?

A. No, I don't.

Q. How are your wrists, by the way, do you play golf?

A. Just a little bit, yes.

Q. Not too good yet, all right. So, to your mind, this is a heavy weapon, isn't that so?

A. Yes.

To further emphasize my physical frailties in this cat-and-mouse game, Hrabsky suddenly picked up the sledgehammer *like a feather*. His big hand hefted it easily and swung it back and forth in front of me. But, having established that the hammer was not heavy, at least in his hands, he knew he still had a problem. To a jury the hammer would still look too massive to have caused slight impressions in Tupper's skull. So Hrabsky turned from muscle-man to legal tactitian. He pointed out that it was true that if the victim was lying down the hammer would crush his skull "down to nothing. But if the victim was standing up, and *dodging*, it would produce only a glancing blow and thus slighter injuries."

That was piling one hypothesis on top of another, I thought. One, that the victim was standing, and, two, that he was nimbly dodging the hammer blows. But such, I knew, was not the case. I told Hrabsky that the lack of blood found in the cranial cavity beneath the wound indicated that the victim was "in the dying stage" and couldn't have dodged anything. If he was alive, his blood would have poured into that cavity and filled it up. In short, the sledgehammer was not the murder weapon.

The defense attorney, on redirect, asked me whether the wounds to the skull could have been caused by a gun butt instead of a sledgehammer, but his question was cut off by a storm of objections. I can say now that I believe Tupper's heads wounds could very well have been caused by something like a gun butt, which would fit with Buddy Jacobsen's theory of a dope rubout, and not a melee in his own apartment in which a construction man was involved.

Later I read in a lively book, *Bad Dreams,* by Anthony Haden-Guest, that Jacobsen had been pleased by my testimony. "That Japanese, he's great!" he is reputed to have said while dining in a restaurant called Nicolas's. I don't know why he thought I had aided his case. My blood-typing tests had not delivered the evidence his defense wished to find. But my sledgehammer testimony might have helped Sal Prainito, the construction worker. He was acquitted.

Much more useful to the defense was a ballistics expert, Shelly Braverman. An expended bullet had been found in the kitchen sink of Leslie Hammond's apartment, which was situated between Jacobsen's and Margarite's. Furthermore, Braverman found a .32 bullet hole in Margarite's closet, and upon placing a probe in its entrance hole he saw that the trajectory pointed straight at the sink.

Braverman also examined two bullet holes in the window of Margarite's apartment and concluded they were made by .32 bullets. The defense claimed that they were stray bullets from a murder which had commenced inside Margarite's apartment, not in Jacobsen's. But, on cross-examination, prosecutor Hrabsky produced a video demonstration which seemed to negate Braverman's testimony about the bullet holes in the window. He ordered a screen placed in the courtroom, then played for the jury a videotape of the holes in the window as they had been photographed by the police immediately after the murder. The size of the holes as seen on the earlier tape was smaller than it was now. Therefore, in the intervening months, the holes must have been enlarged by someone. And that someone, Hrabsky implied, was Buddy Jacobsen when he was out on bail. Forensic forgery, he said, could also account for the bullet hole in Margarite's apartment.

But it was at this time, with his defenses crumbling on all sides, that Buddy Jacobsen had his first stroke of luck. He contacted ballistics expert Herb Mac-Donell and asked him to inspect the corridor on the seventh floor of his building where he, Melanie and Joe Margarite lived. In its far wall there were indentations that Jacobsen believed might be bullet holes. If they were, it supported his claim that drug dealers had finished killing Tupper in the hall, the bullets that had missed hitting the far wall.

As MacDonell told me years later, "I wasn't there to check Melanie Cain's story, only to look at those supposed bullet holes. Well, after examining them, I didn't think they *were* bullet holes—but while I was there, through natural curiosity I noticed something odd."

What MacDonell noticed exploded like a bombshell in court. Melanie's story of that morning's events had survived a withering cross-examination. Now, for the first time, a flaw in her story was exposed. For MacDonell had placed a string from the peephole in her door, past the corner of the wall which jutted out beside it, and found that her line of vision to her left could have included only the elevator. And yet all of the "cover-up" activities by Jacobsen which she had seen, including cutting up the paint-splotched rug, had taken place far beyond the elevator.

The prosecution was obviously caught off guard by

this blow from an unexpected source—a nosy forensic
scientist who, just out of curiosity, had found the first
real suggestion that their star witness might, after all,
not have her facts straight.

They tried to counterattack in two ways. One, they
found a tenant in the building who said that at the
time of the murder all the apartment doors had "fish-
eye" peepholes which allowed a larger field of vision.
Jacobsen, the tenant said, had subsequently replaced
them with old-fashioned tunnel-vision peepholes,
with less scope of sight. Secondly, the prosecution
now said, Melanie had peeked through a *partially
opened door* as well as through the peephole.

In the end, the flaw in Melanie Cain's story was
overwhelmed by all of the other evidence, and on
April 12, 1980, Buddy Jacobsen was found guilty of
murder in the second degree. Spectacular to the end,
Jacobsen dramatically escaped, but was eventually returned and sentenced to twenty-five years in prison.

5

In 1984, while conferring with Herb MacDonell on
the Jean Harris trial, in which he had been a key witness, I asked him about his experience in the Jacobsen case. Although he had never appeared in court,
his extemporaneous forensic test of the peephole had
caused the only bad moments in the trial for Melanie
Cain.

In response to my questions, MacDonell went to his
files and returned with the report he had prepared for
Jacobsen's attorneys—and two items which fascinated me: personal drawings made by Buddy Jacob-

sen himself of the seventh-floor apartments and halls, with his personal handwritten notes indicating points of evidence. The two drawings, one apparently for the use of his attorney and the other for his current girl-friend to do her own ad hoc investigation, were almost identical. They graphically revealed Jacobsen's own theory of the murder: a shooting by drug dealers which culminated in the hall outside Margarite's apartment.

Jacobsen's drawings identified the part of the shooting which took place right outside Margarite's apartment. They showed the trajectory of a stray bullet through Margarite's closet and into the sink of Hammond's apartment, while the other bullets flew straight down the hall, either into Tupper's body or into the far wall. Examining the drawing, I saw an intriguing detail. Jacobsen had drawn footprints beside that far wall and labeled them "Melanie's white paint sneaker prints." The wall, Jacobsen claimed, had been painted to obscure the "bullet holes," and the note revealed who he thought did the painting.

I also noticed that in the drawing of his own apartment made for his girlfriend, Jacobsen had made three circles in the living-room area in which he wrote "I loved you here," "And here," "And here"— three romantic references intended, I suppose, to inspire his girlfriend to Olympian efforts in her investigation.

MacDonell said, "As to the bullet holes in the wall, I couldn't help the defense." He handed me his report, which read, in part:

Due consideration was given to the repainting of the wall ... Without actual test firing into the wall itself, there is no way to determine the similarity of the depressions within this wall and those that might result from impact of a .32 bullet of the same manufacture and fired from the weapon in question. It is my opinion, however, that these depressions were not caused by such impact. Nevertheless, I cannot suggest an alternate as to how they were produced.

"The paint was no problem," MacDonell said. "I made a stereoscopic examination sample from the wall and I found no lead or copper. But while I was in the hallway, I kept looking at Melanie Cain's door —and it didn't add up. I realized she couldn't possibly have seen what she said she had from that door. So, just out of decency for the forensic profession—or plain old curiosity—I included this item in the report I sent to Jacobsen's attorney."

I read further in his report: "Geometry of the apartment door and peephole of Cain's apartment make it impossible for anyone to look out and have vision to any point left of the elevator's left door casing."

"I understand the prosecution went crazy when that information hit them," MacDonell said.

"But what about the prosecution's claim that the peepholes were changed?" I asked. "And also that she peeked from a partially opened door."

"That was a phony defense," MacDonell said. "No matter what kind of peephole, no matter how far the door was open, she couldn't see down the hall, because her door was recessed. A wall abutted the door, and that wall shut off her vision to the side. To see what she said she saw, she would have to have stepped clear out into the open in the middle of the hall. But that wasn't what she testified. And, anyway, look at Buddy Jacobsen's diagram and see where Joe Margarite's door is."

I looked, and observed that Margarite's door was around the corner from the elevator and down the hall. "She couldn't have seen Jacobsen enter Margarite's apartment no matter where she stood," MacDonell said.

In sum, if MacDonell's theory was right, part of Melanie Cain's testimony was wrong, and, friends of Jacobsen said, if she was wrong on one point, why not others—including some of those visits to Jacobsen's apartment and the telephone call from an outdoor booth which the defense had found so suspicious, because they were so convenient for the prosecution?

A month later a friend of mine met a man named Thomas Baratta and relayed his remarks to me. Baratta manages a popular restaurant in Manhattan called Marylou's, but before that he was a hairdresser employed by television-commercial producers. He said that he and his wife were "best friends" with Melanie. Indeed, two days before the murder, while doing a Breck shampoo commercial, Melanie had told them of her fears about the Buddy Jacobsen situation. Nevertheless, Baratta had a surprising comment. He thought Buddy might be innocent. Why? "Because the murder was so *dumb* from beginning to end. And whatever you think of Buddy, he was not stupid."

Another acquaintance of Jacobsen agreed. Standing out in the open at a Bronx dump site beside the body of a man he had murdered? Stupid. Killing Tupper on a morning when the police were on their way to question him about Cheryl Corey's death? Stupid. Murdering Melanie's lover that morning, when Melanie was banging on his door "every ten minutes"? Stupid.

Something is wrong, they feel. Buddy Jacobsen was too smart to have done those things.

My own opinion, after my research, is that there are

many questions in this case yet to be answered. The forensic evidence MacDonell discovered that contradicts parts of Melanie Cain's testimony bothers me, because it raises questions about the rest of her testimony, and the defense in the trial implied that she knew more about the killing than she admitted. On the other hand, she may be responsible only for what Mark Twain used to call a "stretcher" in her testimony about what she saw from her door, and the rest of her story may be accurate. The evidence of violence in Jacobsen's apartment supports her.

Joe Margarite, who disappeared the day of Tupper's murder, finally surfaced in 1982 when he was arrested for allegedly plotting to smuggle Lebanese hashish into the country. Margarite was not considered a suspect in Tupper's slaying, New York police emphasized, but, as Edward McCarthy, a spokesman for the Bronx District Attorney, said, "We believe he has the information that will cause all the pieces of the puzzle to fit together. He is the only one who could fill in all the holes." Authorities always believed that four people were involved in the murder, McCarthy added, but had only enough information to link Jacobsen and another man to the crime. It was later revealed that Margarite had provided the weapons used to kill Tupper, but that was the only additional piece of the puzzle to emerge.

Four people involved in a love-triangle murder? Death weapons provided by a drug dealer? Melanie Cain, according to forensic evidence, caught in an error on the witness stand? To me, it all adds up to a mystery that has yet to be completely solved.

BREAKTHROUGHS IN FORENSIC SCIENCE

No one man can lay claim to the distinction of being called "the father of forensic science." Many men of many nationalities have contributed to this complex profession over the centuries, most of them completely unknown to the public today and, sadly, not even recognized in conventional medical circles. But they were giants who, starting with no precedents or guidelines, possessing only primitive instruments, were able to discover the secrets of the human body, bit by bit, for the use of the law in administering justice, and of physicians in bettering public health.

All forensic science begins with one man, Alphonse Bertillon, an obscure clerk in the Paris Prefecture of Police. Born in 1853, the son of a distinguished physician, Dr. Louis-Adolphe Bertillon, the young Bertillon was bad-tempered, snobbish and pedantic, just to name a few of his less attractive characteristics. Expelled from several schools, fired from various jobs, he was, in all, an unlikely hero for our profession. But, toiling in a remote and shabby corner of the Prefecture, Bertillon could not help but notice the chaos in the police procedures. The central problem was identification of criminals. Because the lawbreakers used aliases and disguises, descriptions and primitive photographs in police card files were worthless. An escaped prisoner could be caught in a new felony, and the police would not even know he was the same man.

Bertillon was fascinated by the problem—and devised two techniques to solve it. First, he standardized the photographic process, making certain that all pictures of criminals would be taken from exactly the same position and with the same lighting. Thus pictures could be compared with some confidence later. He also insisted on one full-face and one profile photo, so that facial features could be better studied, a process still in use in taking police "mug shots" today.

But Bertillon's major contribution to forensic science was what he called anthropometry, and what other scientists soon called "Bertillonage." Bertillon devised a system to *measure* criminals from head to toe. More precisely, he measured certain components of their bodies, such as length and breadth of their heads, lengths of their middle fingers, lengths of their left feet and so on—all of which remained constant throughout their adult lives. He calculated that the chance of two persons having the exact measurements of these several components was more than four million to one.

Soon anthropometrics was adopted by police systems around the world. But, ironically, "Bertillonage" was already on its way out almost as soon as it was installed. For two men, one an Englishman in India, William Herschel, and the other a Scottish physician in Tokyo, Henry Faulds, at almost the same time, happened to notice an oddity: all fingerprints are unique.

Bertillon's measurement technique was time-consuming and relied for accuracy on the persons who made the measurements. The fingerprinting technique was simple and fast, and it guaranteed identification. Nevertheless, the process was held back for decades because no one could figure out how to classify fingerprints so that they could be stored on file cards. Finally, an Englishman named Francis Galton, a cousin of Charles Darwin, conceived a technique of discerning four patterns, based on a triangular figure called the delta, which appeared on almost every fingertip. Galton classified fingerprints as to whether they contained no triangle, a triangle on the right or left, or several triangles. With modification, his technique is still in use today.

Although anthropometry soon fell into disfavor, Bertillon made another major contribution to forensic science by establishing the world's first criminalistics laboratory as a part of the Sûreté. Again he adapted the tools of science to identify physical evidence found at the scene to help determine the cause and circumstance of death. Still, the primary source of evidence was the body itself. For example, a Roman physician named Antistius examined the corpse of Julius Caesar after death, counted twenty-three wounds, and announced that only one stab wound in the chest had been fatal. (Whether that wound was inflicted by Brutus was either not known or not said.) But for centuries there were no autopsies as we know them today. "Natural" deaths may not have been natural at all, while in cases of "unnatural death" physicians would merely widen the wounds of victims to examine the depth and penetration of weapons.

Possibly the first autopsy was performed in Italy by a Belgian, Andreas Vesalius, an anatomist in the sixteenth century who dissected cadavers to learn the secrets of the human body for medical purposes, not to aid the law. Later in the century an Italian, Fidelis, performed the first *forensic* autopsies on drowning victims, trying to differentiate between a murder and an accidental drowning. And, at about the same time, a Frenchman, Ambroise Paré, conducted autopsies intended to discover the effects of violence on the inner organs of the body.

The founder of the science of pathology was an eighteenth-century Italian named Giovanni Battista Morgagni, who made a complete study of the internal organs of the body looking for symptoms of the disease that had caused death. Later, with the invention of the microscope, pathologists would discover the hitherto invisible human cell as the basic unit of the body, and further technological inventions would lead to other discoveries of the causes of death.

In 1901 a German professor named Paul Uhlenhuth made a remarkable contribution to forensic science: the identification of blood from analysis of bloodstains. Uhlenhuth found that the blood serum (the watery component of the blood) could be used to distinguish between human and animal blood by the way it reacted to a sample of each in laboratory tests. He was then able to scrape off dried bloodstains, liquify them in a saline solution, and determine whether the blood was human or animal in origin. The first great step in bloodstain identification had been taken.

On another forensic front, Dr. Paul Browarded in 1897 published the first major study which distinguished deaths by hanging from those by choking. He analyzed the rope marks on the throat of a victim who had been hanged, showing the impression of the knot and the strictures of the skin which would occur. If the victim had been throttled with a cord, the mark ran in a complete circle around the neck. Choking with the hands also left characteristic clues: breaks of the cartilage of the larynx, as well as bruises and sometimes fingernail marks.

In 1925 the first major work in another important field of forensic science, ballistics, was published. *Text Book of Forensic Medicine,* by Dr. Sidney Smith, a New Zealander, covered every aspect of forensic medicine and was the first to include ballistics as part of the science. In those days black powder was used in guns. Smith and other scientists, firing guns at white paper, were able to show the distance of the weapon from the victim. Soot around the bullet wound meant a shot from one-half inch to three inches away. A wound which showed no soot but contained unburned particles of powder indicated a shot up to three feet in distance. In a direct contact wound, both soot and unburned powder were found, together with a blistering of the skin caused by exploding gases from the gun muzzle.

In later years smokeless powder came into use, with traces more difficult to detect. But by then forensic science had developed devices which could detect such traces, even when almost invisible. Further, those devices could analyze the physical components such as lead and antimony and tell police authorities the type and caliber of the ammunition and the weapon, a great aid to detectives investigating a murder.

In 1889 Professor Alexandre Lacassagne, a Frenchman, had pioneered in another phase of ballistics, the examination of the bullet itself. While an analysis of bullet fragments could identify the types of ammunition and gun, bullet analysis could identify the particular gun as distinguished from all others, much like fingerprinting. Lacassagne noticed seven longitudinal marks on a bullet he found in the body of a shooting victim. He checked a local gunsmith in Lyons and discovered that different guns from various manufacturers had different riflings—the spiral grooves cut into the inner surface of the barrel. The number of grooves would vary, as well as their width and the number of their windings.

Soon, forensic scientists began test-firing weapons to compare their bullets with those found in victims or at the scenes of crimes. And they made a remarkable discovery. Not only did the rifling of the guns vary, as Lacassagne had found, from manufacturer to manufacturer, but from gun to gun. Under the microscope, and later the comparison microscope, it was seen that the rifling of each gun was unique. The cutting machines that made the rifling created minute differences in each boring of a gun, differences that could be observed only under magnification. Thus it was possible by examining a bullet to identify with even greater precision the gun that had fired it. And these principles still guide the profession of ballistics today.

The investigation of unexplained deaths by fire was the province of another pioneer, an Austrian named Schwarzocher. With only a charred body as evidence, how could you distinguish between an accidental burning and murder by burning, or even murder in which the already dead victim was set afire to conceal a crime?

Schwarzocher found that those who were burned alive inhaled soot and carbon monoxide, caused by the combustion of the fire. The soot would be detected in the lungs, and the carbon monoxide in the blood, clues which almost always meant an accidental burning. Murder by burning alive, on the other hand, would often leave clues which indicated violence, even though the body was charred on the outside. For one thing, strangulation marks could be seen even after the fire. For another, it was believed that violence caused fat to be expelled from tissues into the blood. These tiny globules of fat emigrated to the heart, and then into the lungs, where they would be found in the corpse. Finally, in the victim who was killed first and then burned, the crime could be detected easily because no soot or carbon monoxide would be found in the lungs and the blood.

For centuries, poison has been a favorite weapon of murderers, including the infamous Borgias. And of these poisons, arsenous oxide, a tasteless, odorless white powder derived from arsenic, was the favorite. The symptoms of the poisoning were identical to those of cholera and other diseases prevalent at that time.

To combat murder by poison, a new science was founded in 1813 by Mathieu Orfila, who is now known to us as the father of toxicology. Orfila, a Spaniard who had moved to Paris, conducted numerous experiments with arsenic on animals so that he could see where the poison traveled in the body, and thus where it could be discovered in internal organs.

But sometimes the arsenic was impossible to trace, and seemed to have vanished. Orfila lacked a means of finding such invisible arsenic until an Englishman named James Marsh conducted an experiment. He mixed sulfuric acid with arsenic, producing a hydrogen gas containing arsenic elements. This gas was ignited as it left the mouth of a test tube while Marsh held a dish above it. The black deposit created on the

dish was pure arsenic. When Marsh placed in his tube
tissues in which arsenic was invisible, the arsenic
would become visible, and toxicology could thereafter detect the presence of the poison in the body of
a victim.

Arsenic is a metallic poison. Even more difficult to
detect are poisons from vegetables and from exotic
plants. Because their chemical basis is alkali, they
were named alkaloids. And one after another of such
alkaloids were isolated—morphine, nicotine, strych-
nine, caffeine, eventually a list of thousands. The alkaloids worked on the nervous system and left no
traces at all in the bodies of the victims that could be
detected by scientists in the early 1800s. Experiment-
ing with these poisons, however, toxicologists of the
day mixed them with various reagents and noted that
each produced a separate color. In addition, many of
them formed crystals whose shapes characterized the
poisons. Next toxicologists found that when the crystals were placed over a fire, most alkaloid poisons had
different melting points. Thus their presence in the
body could also be detected.

The effort to identify alkaloids took on greater in-
tensity as the years progressed, because now toxicologists were searching not only for poisons used in
murder, but for synthetic alkaloids developed by drug
manufacturers to heal, cure or ease the pain of various
maladies, from insomnia to headaches. Unfortunately,
these alkaloids could also be used to commit suicide
or could result in accidental death when ingested in
too great a quantity. Then in 1906 a Russian physicist,
Isvett, reported that dyes traveling down a chalk col-
umn separated according to color, each one stopping
at a different point in the tube. He called his discovery chromatography, which means, in Greek, color

writing. Soon his discovery was taken up by toxicologists as a means of identifying alkaloids by coloring
them with reagents that produced certain colors.
Since then ultraviolet light and, later, electronic devices came into use to aid us in our search for these
deadly poisons.

A pretty ladyfriend of a professor named Adolf Bae-
zer in Berlin in 1864 gave her name to a chemical
composition which has caused hundreds of thousands
of deaths. Her name was Barbara; the substance was
barbituric acid. Physicians found it useful as a sedative, and the toll of suicides from barbituric acid
began almost immediately to rise, as did accidental
deaths and even, occasionally, homicides.

Today, more than a hundred years later, the number
of unexplained deaths from all causes continues to
sprial upward as we forensic scientists struggle to
keep pace. The great scientific breakthroughs made
by our pioneers have given us the principles of forensic analysis in every field, and have led to the development of sophisticated devices embodying these
principles. But the war goes on, and in the following
pages I will describe various battles in that war,
deaths which were a mystery, and murders in which
cunning killers could not be found, until forensic science analyzed the evidence and provided the answers.

A CURIOUS CAUSE OF DEATH
The Case of Dorothy Dandridge

1

Dorothy Dandridge was one of the first great black entertainment stars to emerge in motion pictures. Often compared to Lena Horne, Dorothy was beautiful and possessed a lilting voice that delighted audiences everywhere. Born in Cleveland, Ohio, in 1923, the daughter of a minister, she began her singing career at the age of four. She and her sister, Vivian, were billed as "The Wonder Children" and played in small clubs in the area.

As Dorothy approached adulthood, her beauty was evident to all, and the little girl from Cleveland made the journey to Hollywood. In those days of discrimination, the forties, blacks were almost always either relegated to "Stepin Fetchit" roles or clumped together in all-black films. Nevertheless, Dorothy was special, and she appeared in a legendary Marx Brothers film, *A Day at the Races.*

In the fifties, she reached the zenith of her career, starring in two classics for director Otto Preminger, *Carmen Jones,* a black, jazzy version of Bizet's opera *Carmen,* and *Porgy and Bess,* the great musical drama written by George Gershwin. She won an Academy Award nomination for her role in *Carmen Jones.* At the same time she was one of this country's premiere nightclub entertainers, commanding huge fees in Las Vegas, Miami and other expensive resorts.

But a hint of the discrimination that Dorothy faced in those years would emerge later, in 1957, when she sued a scandal magazine, *Confidential,* over an article provocatively titled "What Dorothy Dandridge Did in the Woods." The story alleged a love tryst with a white bandleader, Daniel Terry, during a two-week singing engagement at Lake Tahoe in 1950. In her suit, Dorothy pointed out that there were "restrictions on Negroes" at the resort which limited her social activities with whites, and she was "never alone" with a white man.

But by the early sixties, discrimination of all kinds in America had eased, and Dorothy should have been poised for even greater successes. Instead, her personal life brought her disaster. Twice she tried marriage; both times the marriages failed. Even more disastrously, she lost all the money she had saved over the years of work in a get-rich-quick oil investment that turned sour. In 1963 she was forced to declare bankruptcy, citing debts of $127,000.

Two years later, on May 21, 1965, Dorothy Dandridge handed a note to her manager, Earl Mills. It read: "In case of my death—to whoever discovers it —Don't remove anything I have on—scarf, gown, or underwear—cremate me right away—If I have anything, money, furniture, give it to my brother." Mills later said Dandridge told him at the time, "You keep the note, Earl, because I know you will be the one who discovers me."

The note certainly suggested that the famed black singer was contemplating suicide. But by September 1, 1965, things were looking up for Dandridge. Her manager took her to Oaxaca, Mexico, where she signed to play in two films for Mexican producer Raúl Fernández. And she was set for a singing engagement in New York's most prestigious jazz club, Basin Street East, beginning September 9.

One day before that engagement, Mills telephoned Dandridge's second-floor apartment at 8405 Fountain Avenue in West Hollywood. She didn't answer, and by 2 P.M. he was worried and went to the address. He found her apartment door unlocked, but bolted by a chain. He used a crowbar borrowed from the building manager to pry the chain lock loose.

Inside he found Dorothy Dandridge in bed clad in a light-blue nightgown. There was no pulse, no heartbeat. She had apparently died in her sleep.

2

The Dorothy Dandrige case was a human tragedy: a talented young black struggling against all odds to achieve success, then having its fruits snatched away, but fighting back, anyway, to rebuild her life—all to end in sudden death. But in my years in the Los Angeles coroner's office, it is remembered for another reason. It sparked one of the most heated scientific controversies ever to occur in our office.

As a deputy medical examiner under Dr. Theodore Curphey, I found myself embroiled in that controversy. The autopsy surgeon's verdict stated that Dandridge had died from a rare medical phenomenon. It seemed that she had sustained a broken toe a few weeks before her death. The autopsy surgeon believed that the accident to the toe released fat from its bone which traveled to the lung and plugged the blood vessels so that the blood could not be oxygenated. Therefore he ruled that the death was caused by a pulmonary fat embolism.

This type of fat, as pathologists know, has its origins as bone marrow, the spongelike substance within the bones of the body which produces red and white blood cells, as well as platelets. The white cells are the fighting soldiers against infection. The platelets produce blood clotting in case of injury. The seeds of these blood cells mature and multiply in the marrow, then are released to general circulation in the blood-stream. Bone marrow is present in all persons during their youth, but when they reach adulthood the marrow in most bones (except spine, ribs, breastbone and pelvis) turns to fat. It was this fat from a broken toe bone which the autopsy surgeon believed to be the cause of Dorothy Dandridge's death.

It was an extraordinary theory, many pathologists in our office believed, myself included. Pulmonary fat embolisms occur because of fractured bones such as the thigh or the shin—but from the toe? There couldn't be more than a teaspoonful of fat in the toe, we thought. What little evidence was available, we believed, pointed to suicide.

Others in the office backed the autopsy surgeon, and arguments raged. On that side of the controversy was a unique sociological fact: suicide is very rare among blacks. Sociologists theorize that they are more resigned to the vicissitudes of life which sometimes tempt Caucasians to suicide. Blacks learn early to endure hardships and shrug them off.

Arguments among the staff over the cause of death are a rare phenomenon nowadays in medical examiners' offices because sophisticated equipment enables us more precisely to prove the truth or falsity of most scientific theories. But in those days, the Los Angeles coroner's office did not have such sophisticated devices. The toxicology laboratory, for example, consisted of only a few test tubes and one old-fashioned gas chromatography device. With these instruments the toxicologist was unable to discover any toxic drugs present in Dandridge's blood.

Thus Dr. Curphey, despite his own doubts, signed the autopsy report which stated that Dandridge's death had occurred because of a pulmonary embolism. But then he took an additional step to resolve the conflict. He sent the liver, the kidney and samples of blood to the Armed Forces Institute of Pathology, which did have sophisticated toxicology devices. There Dr. Leo Goldbaum analyzed the organs and the blood samples and discovered a fatal level of a tranquilizer drug in Dandridge's body fluids.

On November 17, 1965, Dr. Curphey announced that the department was revising its earlier report, a very rare occurrence. It now ruled that Dorothy Dandridge had died from an overdose of drugs—and not from a broken toe.

Partially because of that broken toe, Los Angeles would soon have a modern toxicology laboratory, as all of us on the staff realized how vital such a laboratory was in our work. When I became Chief Medical Examiner in 1969, and we built our new Forensic Science Center, the toxicology laboratory was one of our first priorities.

THE VISIBLE AND INVISIBLE MURDERER
The Case of Sal Mineo

1

Murder is surprisingly rare in the motion picture community, although decidedly *not* rare in the rest of Los Angeles. Perhaps because stardom brings great wealth, enabling actors, producers and directors to reside in Bel-Air and Beverly Hills in homes which resemble fortresses with elaborate security devices, the ugly act of murder does not occur as often as in other communities.

In fact, in my experience, I recall only four cases of homicide among actors and actresses: Ramon Novarro, a Latin actor killed by two homosexual hustlers; Sharon Tate, murdered by the Manson cult; Dorothy Stratten, shot by the husband she was leaving; and Sal Mineo, the young actor from the Bronx, who was stabbed in an alley behind his apartment house by a then unknown assailant. Of the four, the Mineo case is of interest to coroners everywhere because forensic science tripped up a murderer with an apparently ironclad alibi based on what eyewitnesses at the scene of the crime told police.

2

Salvatore Mineo, Jr., was born on January 10, 1939, the son of an Italian-born coffin maker. His Bronx neighborhood, East 217th Street, was tough, and at the age of eight he was already a member of a street gang—and he had been expelled from a parochial school as a troublemaker.

His mother, Josephine, met the challenge in an unusual way. She enrolled her son in a dancing class. Three years later, when Mineo was eleven, Broadway producer Cheryl Crawford, who was searching for two Italian-American children to play bit parts in Tennessee Williams' *The Rose Tattoo,* saw Mineo in dancing school. Crawford asked the boy to recite the line "The goat is in the yard."

That turned out to be Mineo's line in the play; in fact, most of his acting ability in the play was focused on the chore of leading a balky goat across the stage of the Martin Beck Theatre night after night for a year. But the exposure won him entrance to the world of show business—and a real acting job as the young prince in *The King and I.*

By the age of fiteen, Sal Mineo was in Hollywood, and at seventeen, in 1956, he won an Academy Award as a troubled juvenile in *Rebel Without a Cause.* The movie established Mineo as a teenage idol, along with his co-stars, Natalie Wood and James Dean. They too were to die untimely deaths, Dean in a car accident in 1955, at the height of his film career, and Wood in 1981 in the sea off Catalina Island.

In 1961 Mineo won a second Academy Award nomination, this time for his role as Dov Landau, a survivor of a Nazi concentration camp turned into a Zionist terrorist, in *Exodus.* A close relationship with his teenage co-star, Jill Haworth, followed. But then, as so often happens in Hollywood, the magic suddenly dissolved. Good roles did not come Mineo's way, perhaps because the tough young delinquents of the fifties were no longer in style. By the 1960s the "rebels without a cause" were college students *with* a cause, to end the Vietnam War. Mineo was reduced to playing television roles in shows such as *Ellery Queen* and *Joe Forrester,* and his only role in a major motion picture was as an ape in *Escape from the Planet of the Apes.*

Through this decline, as his close friend the director Peter Bogdanovich wrote, Mineo never complained. Instead he retained his "sunny and easygoing qualities, his quick wit and infectious self-mockery." And by 1969, with his image as a teenage "punk" far behind him, and with film roles for an adult Mineo scarce, he returned to his first great love, the theater. In that year he directed *Fortune and Men's Eyes,* which opened in Los Angeles and proved a great success, eventually moving to Broadway in New York.

The play had a homosexual background, as did Mineo's role in *P.S. Your Cat Is Dead,* in which he was to star in 1976. On the night of February 12 of that year, Salvatore Mineo, Jr., returned to his apartment house from a rehearsal and parked his blue Chevelle in a carport in the rear. At that moment, his assailant struck. Neighbors heard Mineo cry out, "Oh God, no! Help! Someone help!" Then they heard sounds of a struggle, more screams, then silence.

Seconds later, bystanders saw a man fleeing down the driveway and speeding off in a car—a white man with long brown hair, they later told police. By the time they reached the thirty-seven-year-old Mineo, he was near death, a long stream of blood flowing from a stab wound in his chest. A neighbor, Roy Evans, gave him mouth-to-mouth resuscitation. "He kept gasping and after about five minutes his last breath went into me," Evans said later, "and that was the end of it."

But it was the beginning of the mystery—and the rumors about the actor's death. As *Newsweek* magazine reported:

> Police investigators were unable to establish any motive for the killing—there was no evidence of robbery. But partly because of Mineo's recent homosexual roles and partly because the knifing occurred near the notoriously kinky Sunset Strip, long whispered reports of the actor's alleged bisexuality and fondness for sadomasochistic ritual quickly surrounded his murder.

As the Chief Medical Examiner of Los Angeles County, I supervised the autopsy of Sal Mineo's body, which was performed with his usual care and excellence by Dr. Manuel R. Breton, one of my deputy medical examiners. The killer has escaped, but perhaps, we thought, the body of his victim would present clues to us. So our first step was to X-ray the lower chest and the upper abdomen to see if any metallic fragments from the knife could be found. There were none. Our second step was to preserve evidence of the exact nature of the fatal wound. In the prosaic words of the autopsy report, our forensic-science decision read this way: "Sections: 1. For storage: routine representative sections of main tissue and organs, including stab wound of the skin and heart, are submitted. . . ."

That precaution was to prove the undoing of the anonymous murderer.

3

For more than a year, police pursued every lead in the Mineo case without success, until it was reported to them that a convict in Michigan named Lionel Williams had been overheard telling another prisoner, "Have you ever killed anybody? It's very easy." A guard, Albert Lemkuhl, told police that Williams had boasted of killing Mineo.

The reason the police were talking to guards and prisoners about Williams was that his wife in Los Angeles, Theresa, had fingered him for the murder of Sal Mineo. Mrs. Williams said that her husband had returned home on the night of the killing covered with blood, saying, "I just killed this dude in Hollywood." Williams told his wife that he had murdered Mineo with a hunting knife.

In the Michigan jail, where he was now imprisoned on a $174 bad-check charge, Williams denied telling the guard he had killed Mineo. But police noticed an unusual tattoo on his arm: a hunting knife. As the police said, "It was almost as if he put the mark of Cain on himself."

Concentrating their investigation on Williams, the police soon found evidence of a whole chain of vicious muggings in Los Angeles allegedly committed by Williams. Could the murder of Mineo have been the result of a routine mugging? A witness said the getaway car was a yellow subcompact; police discovered a loan agreement showing that Williams was driving a yellow Dodge Colt on the night of the murder.

The web of circumstantial evidence began to pin Williams tighter, except for one startling fact. Williams was a black man with an Afro hairdo. Every witness in the area had seen a *white* man run from the scene.

It was then the police remembered the chest section stored in the Los Angeles County Forensic Science Center, in which the stab wound was preserved.

When a stab wound causes a fatal injury, we always examine that wound for several characteristics such as length, width, thickness, single-edge blade or double, sharp or dull. By surgical procedure we also examine the wound layer by layer.

In effect we create what I call a "negative cast," which is the wound itself and which is preserved in its surrounding tissues in formalin. Our goal is to provide a precise means of identifying the murder weapon, if it is recovered, by matching the wound with the knife.

At the time of the Mineo murder, we had purchased a number of knives to assist our research into stab wounds, because deaths from slashers had become prevalent in Los Angeles. When the police arrived at our office they had a description obtained from Williams' wife of a hunting knife owned by Williams. She even knew its price: $5.28. We had an exactly similar knife in our collection.

Normally we don't insert an allegedly matching knife into a wound during an autopsy, because it would distort the incision. But now, because the tissues had been fixed in formalin for storage, we could do so without such distortion. We inserted the blade of this knife into the wound, and it matched perfectly.

Still, the owner of the knife was black, and eyewitnesses had seen a white man fleeing from the scene.

It was then that police discovered in their files a photograph of Williams taken by them a few years before, when he had been suspected of another crime, and suddenly we had our solution to the mystery. The picture showed that Williams did not have an Afro at that time. Instead, he had long, "processed" hair which was light brown and worn in the style of Caucasians. That was the way he had looked on the night of Mineo's murder, and the witnesses had been wrong. The long brown hair, unusual for blacks, had fooled them.

Eyewitness accounts, as police and medical examiners know, can be notoriously inaccurate, a constant problem for the courts. In the death of Sal Mineo, they presented a seemingly insoluble obstacle to the prosecution. Nevertheless, excellent police work, assisted by forensic science, brought the killer to justice.

ONE LAST LAUGH
The Case of Freddie Prinze

1

A strange Hollywood case that was handled by the Medical Examiner's Office during my tenure as its chief was that of Freddie Prinze, the sensational young Latino star of a hit television show, *Chico and the Man*, who, at the peak of his success and fame, put a gun to his head and shot himself.

Freddie Prinze was born June 22, 1954, in a Span-
ish-speaking area of Washington Heights near Harlem
which the comic actor later described as "a slum with
trees." From the first he had an identity problem in
the neighborhood because his father was a Hungarian
Jew. Prinze called himself a Hunga-Rican. Also, as he
recalled, he was "a fat kid, poor at sports, and I had
asthma. I also studied piano and ballet, which tended
to blow my credibility as a tough guy."

But Prinze could make his peers laugh—and that
talent proved to be his ticket out of the ghetto. His
hard-working parents enrolled him in the High
School of Performing Arts in Manhattan. "But actually," Prinze said, "I learned more in the Improvisation Club and on the street than I ever did at
school."

The Improvisation featured young amateur comics
of every kind, and there Prinze developed a routine
with a Latino accent, which was entirely new to the
paying customers. Latino comics were, at the time,
nonexistent in the entertainment world, and so the
crowds roared at his particular ethnic humor:

"My mother's always talking about the wedding.
You shoulda been there, she says. She doesn't remember. I *was* there, and so were my two brothers.

"Each day when I was going to school as a kid my
mother gave me a dollar bill as protection. 'Eef you
get mugged, you geeve him thees!' So, every day I
geeve the mugger the buck, till one rainy day I take a
chance and spend the money on a soda. But the mugger catches me anyway, and when I tell him I don't
have my dollar, he says, indignant, 'I'm gonna tell
your ma!' "

The aspiring comics at the Improvisation worked
for no pay, their only reward the possibility that an

agent or a producer might be in the audience, and one particular night fate smiled on Freddie Prinze. An agent thought he had promise, and bookings at the Playboy Club and on the Jack Paar television program followed.

Quickly, his career snowballed. In 1973 Prinze made an appearance on the Johnny Carson show and scored a great personal success. Carson asked him back several times, and fate kept smiling on Prinze. Television situation comedies at the time employed no Latino actors, but a producer who saw Prinze on *The Tonight Show* happened to be planning the first comedy ever to star a Chicano. Prinze won the role of the young Chicano who worked for a bigoted, hard-drinking old garage owner in East Los Angeles.

The situation comedy was a phenomenal success from the first, never out of the top ten in ratings. Prinze's words to his frustrated boss, "Ees not my chob!" became a national gag line. By 1977 Prinze seemed to have everything going for him. Besides *Chico and the Man,* he had just signed a lucrative contract with Caesar's Palace in Las Vegas. He was negotiating film deals with Warner Brothers and Universal. He had filled in for Johnny Carson as host of *The Tonight Show,* and more such appearances were in the offing. As *Time* magazine reported, "At the age of 22, he attained one of the highest status roles in show business when he performed for the President at the Inaugural Gala in Washington."

That was one month before Freddie Prinze committed suicide.

2

At 3 A.M., January 29, 1977, the telephone rang in the home of Martin "Dusty" Snyder, Prinze's business manager. The actor wanted to talk, but he sounded "strange" to Snyder, who quickly dressed and drove to Prinze's home.

Snyder was worried that the pressure from several areas was getting to his client. Prinze had been commuting between Las Vegas and Hollywood, doing both his nightclub act and the arduous all-day filming of *Chico and the Man,* which left him fatigued. Further, he and Kathy, his wife and the mother of their young son, had separated six months before. Lastly, and most ominously, the actor had become a Quaalude addict.

Quaalude is a brand name for methaqualone hydrochloride, described in physician's terms as a sedative-hypnotic. It is a dangerous drug often implicated in suicides. Addiction leads to such symptoms as loss of memory, inability to concentrate, tremors and finally depression.

But when Snyder appeared at Prinze's house, the actor didn't seem disturbed; instead Prinze greeted him at the door with a smile. Dressed in his favorite karate pants, he went to the sofa while Snyder sat in a nearby loveseat. Prinze wrote something on a piece of notepaper, then pushed it across the coffee table to Snyder, saying, "Is that legible?"

Snyder read the words "I cannot go on any longer." Before he could reply, Prinze picked up the telephone and called his estranged wife. In that conversation he informed her that he was going to "end it all," but Snyder didn't hear this as he quietly slipped out of the room to telephone Prinze's psychiatrist, Dr. William S. Kroger, and ask what to do.

Dr. Kroger reportedly replied, "He's been behaving this way all this week. He's just crying out for attention and help, but I'm not concerned with his doing harm to himself."

When Snyder returned, he found Prinze now on the phone to his secretary, Carol Novak. By the end of that call, the actor seemed to relax, quietly bending over the coffee table and adding more words to the note that he had written.

Finished, he put the pen down, then suddenly reached under a sofa cushion and pulled out a revolver. Instinctively Snyder reached out to grab it, but Prinze gestured with the gun for Snyder to sit back. Snyder talked desperately to Prinze. He reminded him of his mother and his baby, and that his insurance policy had a suicide clause which would mean they wouldn't get the money.

Prinze listened, but then pressed the muzzle of the gun against his temple and squeezed the trigger.

The close contact muted the sound, but the results were catastrophic. Blood spattered everywhere as the twenty-two-year-old actor toppled sideways on the sofa, dead.

3

Prinze's body was brought to our Forensic Science Center, and a week later, as I studied the autopsy report, I was worried. On its face, Prinze's death was one of the most obvious suicides in my experience. Not only had he shot himself in front of an eyewitness a few feet away, but he had telephoned both his estranged wife and his secretary to inform them he was going to do so. Further, he had written a suicide note and handed it to Snyder. And finally, his blood revealed a high level of Quaaludes, which causes suicidal depression.

And yet, I was puzzled by one factor: a witness had been present. In my long and sad experience with suicides, victims almost always perform the act in solitude. Prinze had committed suicide in front of a friend. Why?

I remember telling associates that I expected trouble in this case. In fact, I called Dr. Robert Litman, the suicide psychology expert, to discuss the matter. Taking all the facts into consideration, however, including the telephone call to his ex-wife, and the other circumstantial and eyewitness evidence of a suicide, which was overwhelming, we both believed Prinze's death was by suicide, and that was the coroner's official verdict.

But a few months later I received my first hint that my earlier concerns had been correct. An attorney for Prinze's mother called me and said the family would claim that Prinze's death was an accident, not a suicide. As insurance money was involved, I wasn't surprised by the action. Nor was I surprised that there might have been another aspect to Prinze's death. But I asked the attorney how he intended to prove that it was not suicide.

In reply, he informed me that on the very day of his death Prinze, while high on Quaaludes, had waved the gun in front of his secretary, Carol Novak, in his apartment, pulled the trigger, then collapsed to the floor. When Novak rushed to his side in horror, the actor sat up, laughing.

According to both Carol Novak and Prinze's psychiatrist, Dr. Kroger, Prinze had been fooling around with the gun for some time, "showing off." The family was going to claim in court that his death was not a suicide but, instead, an accident that had occurred while Prinze, under the influence of Quaaludes, was showing off or playing a prank, and forgot that the safety was off.

On January 20, 1983, the family's claim was upheld by a jury, and $200,000 in insurance money was paid to them. The attorney said afterward, "It has been the mother's feeling in her heart and in her mind that Freddie did not intend to commit suicide; that if it had not been for the drugs he would not have done what he did."

Collaterally, Prinze's widow and son, in 1981 and 1982, had won almost one million dollars in settlement of malpractice suits against Prinze's psychiatrist, Dr. Kroger, and his internist, Dr. Edward B. Albon. Those suits claimed that Kroger had improperly allowed Prinze access to the gun he used to kill himself, after once taking it away, and that Albon had wrongly overprescribed Quaaludes.

Thus, in the eyes of the law, the man who shot himself in front of an eyewitness turned out not to be a suicide. The actual cause of death, whether by suicide or by accident, was a drug, Quaalude. And so, in reality, Freddie Prinze did not die by his own hand. He died in one last tragic attempt to get a laugh.

MURDER IN HOLLYWOOD
The Case of Dorothy Stratten

1

Rapes which climax in murder are a continuing affliction of our society. To counter this affliction, I set up a Sexual Assault Evidence Data Processing Unit in our Forensic Science Center in Los Angeles. Evidence collected by this unit aids the Los Angeles Police Department in many ways, from establishing the motive for a killing to actually identifying the murderer.

For example, the first item in the Sexual Assault Evidence Data sheet, under "General Evidence Collection," is "Nail Scrapings Collected." In a rape the victim often claws or scratches her assailant's face and body. But even though police might suspect a man whose face bears such a scratch, the suspect will always claim he received the wound in an innocent matter.

Forensic science can prove it *was* made by the victim. I remember particularly a case in which a pretty young girl was found dead, her dress in disarray above her thighs. Her throat had been cut, and there was evidence of semen in her vagina. In sum, an obvious rape/murder. When LAPD detectives questioned her boyfriend, they noticed he had a small scratch on his cheek, but it was so small it could have come from shaving, as the suspect insisted. However, our scientists had preserved a tiny roll of skin found under one of the victim's fingernails. They rolled it flat—and it exactly fit the scratch on the suspect's face. That led to intensive interrogation, and he eventually confessed to the murder.

Another important item under "General Evidence Collection" is "Bite Mark Evidence." Sexual assailants sometimes bite their victims, and forensic dentistry can now reconstruct the teeth of the murderer from such a bite mark. The most famous case of bite-mark identification occurred in Florida, where, at long last, a serial killer named Theodore Bundy was apprehended.

Bundy, a clean-cut, attractive man of about thirty, began his killing spree in the Northwest. He had a specialty: beautiful college girls with long dark hair. He would approach these coeds, lure them into his car, rape and kill them, then toss them into a lonely area of the forest. By the time their bodies were discovered, they had been ravaged by animals and insects and provided no clues to investigators.

After a series of such murders, Bundy moved on to a Southwestern college and murdered several girls there. Then—always on the move to further confuse and frustrate detectives—he went all the way to Florida. But there one night at a Miami college he altered his usual pattern. Instead of luring one of the coeds into his car, he invaded her room in a small dormitory, raped and killed her, then did the same to her two roommates when they returned unexpectedly.

No doubt, continuing his *modus operandi*, he would have left Florida and started a new round of killings in a distant state—but he had at last made one mistake in his continuing orgy of murders. He bit the buttock of one of his victims. And then, fleeing the scene, he was stopped for a traffic violation by police in Tampa, who noted that his driver's license was a forgery. While he was being questioned, news of the deaths in Miami and the missing murderer came through.

There was other evidence against Bundy, but none as conclusive as the reconstruction of his teeth that forensic dentists were able to make from that single bite mark found on one of his victims. Introduced in court as evidence, it matched Bundy's teeth perfectly. He was convicted of murder, and a serial killer was stopped in his rampage, because of a bite—and forensic science.

Forensic science has many tools besides dentistry to investigate rape/murders, from microscopy and serology, which detect spermatozoa, to ballistics, which identifies firearms employed, to psychology, which seeks to profile the killer. All of these factors came together one day in the investigation of a crime in Hollywood which shocked the nation.

2

A beautiful girl lies dead of a shotgun wound. A young man lies near her, also killed by a shotgun, which is on the floor near his feet. A double murder by an intruder, or murder followed by a suicide?

That was the actual scene of the death of Dorothy Stratten, a "small town" girl who had come to Hollywood to pursue a career as a model and actress. The dead young man was Paul Snider, her hometown boyfriend, later her husband, and their tragic story began in Vancouver, Canada, where Dorothy Hoogstraaten was serving ice cream cones at a Dairy Queen when a young man with a mustache and trendy jeans entered.

Paul Snider ordered a cone and studied the fresh-complexioned, voluptuous young girl, and saw what he had been looking for: a potential Playmate for *Playboy* magazine.

The magazine offered thousands of dollars to those girls willing to bare their bodies for *Playboy*'s readers. The young woman behind the counter was the perfect girl-next-door type that the magazine craved—and Snider could get a commission. He told Dorothy he was a promoter and "producer," persuaded her to go to dinner with him, and a romance blossomed. With one catch. Dorothy refused to take her clothes off before the camera. But eventually Snider prevailed, the pictures were sent to *Playboy*, and it is a tribute to Dorothy Stratten's beauty that less than two days after *Playboy* received them she was on her way to Hollywood.

Hugh Hefner's Playboy Mansion is a notorious part of the Hollywood scene, crowded with lovely young girls and often visited by male Hollywood stars, directors and producers. Stratten was moved right into the house. Hefner, the founder of *Playboy,* told her she might be not only a Playmate of the Year, but a candidate for the Playmate of the Quarter-Century. Snider, elated with her success, flew down to Los Angeles, where he announced to Hefner that he was Dorothy's manager.

According to reports, Hefner did not like Snider, whom he described as a small-time hustler. Worse for Snider, Hefner introduced the naive young beauty to Peter Bogdanovich, a skilled and respected motion picture director, who had seen his career founder through his love for another young model and actress, Cybill Shepherd. He had cast Shepherd in certain expensive movies for which her talents were apparently not suited, and in the end both Shepherd and his career had gone into temporary eclipse.

Nevertheless, such was the beauty of this young girl from Vancouver that Bogdanovich felt himself fatally attracted again. He cast Dorothy in a movie he was making in New York, and once the two were on location in the city they fell in love.

Meanwhile, Snider's world was falling apart. Determined to cash in on Dorothy's success, he had earlier persuaded her to marry him, thus strengthening his hold on her. But now he felt he was losing her. He had also been barred from the Playboy Mansion—the ultimate snub to someone of Snider's makeup. Rejected and humiliated, he decided to take action. When Dorothy returned from New York, she did not move in with him. She wanted a divorce. Snider hired a private detective to follow her.

On August 15, 1980, the private investigator alerted friends of Snider's who lived above him to the fact that neither Snider nor Stratten had emerged from Snider's apartment after a meeting in which they were supposed to thrash out their problems. Within minutes a dreadful scene was discovered in that apartment, and an investigator from the coroner's office, Michael A. Shepherd, was on his way to the scene.

3

When I became Chief Medical Examiner in 1967 there was no full-time investigator's staff in the coroner's office. I installed such a staff, and it has done excellent work through the years. Skilled investigators who can go to the scene of a crime, search it professionally for clues to the cause and circumstance of death, collect vital evidence, and make a detailed report of all criminalistic and other relevant factors at the scene are now an integral part of the forensic process.

In the Stratten case, investigator Shepherd filed a particularly excellent description and forensic analysis of the scene.

Decedents are a 20-year-old female and 20-year-old male, who are married, but separated, pending divorce action. Decedent 80-10485 is the 1980 Playmate of the Year (professional name: Dorothy Stratten). Decedent 80-10486 is her husband. . . .

Coroner observed both Decedents in a first floor bedroom. Both were unclothed, both in full rigor. Decedent Hoogstraaten, 80-10485, was cool to the touch, lying semi-crouched across the end of a low bed . . . She was lying with both legs on the carpet, and right shoulder on the carpet, with her buttocks raised. She had blood stains, possible hand prints, to her buttocks, and left leg. She had trauma to both knees. She had an entrance [wound], close to the contact shotgun wound to her left cheek, with much blood loss. She had lividity consistent with her position. She had non-consistent blood stains to her left shoulder and left arm. There was blood splatter on the east wall and curtains, next to her head. She had lost the tip of her left index finger, possible gunshot wound. Beneath her was a towel, with a hole and blood stains.

Near Decedent Hoogstraaten's head, but at an angle away from her, a "love seat" sexual appliance was on the floor. It was set into a position for possible rear entry intercourse.

Decedent Snider, 80-10486, was cool to the touch, lying prone on the rug, lying head to the east, in line with the end of the bed . . . He was lying with both hands beneath him, at lower chest level. A shotgun was observed under him, lying under Decedent, stock toward his neck, barrel toward the right knee. He had an entrance shotgun wound to the right side of his head, with open wound between his eyes, and drain from the wound behind his left ear. The left eye was bulging from the socket. His right hand had long blond hair in it (recovered by Coroner in Miscellaneous Evidence). The wound to the right side of his head had a blackened portion about it. . . .

Decedent's right index finger was extended, with the rest of the right fingers curled. The fingers of the left hand were curled. Lividity matched his position, to include an outline of the shotgun. He had trauma to his right thumb. An expended round of 12 gauge #4 buckshot load was recovered from the weapon, a 12 gauge Mossberg pump shotgun. It is two feet-two inches from the depressed position of the trigger to the end of the barrel.

An expended round of similar type and an unexpended round were recovered from the floor, about both bodies.

At this time, no notes were found. A tape recorder was checked at the scene, with negative results. At this point, no one has come forth with statements of intent of action or frame of mind of violent action, by either Decedent, toward the other Decedent.

To the layman, such a report might seem shocking and chillingly impersonal, but it is essential in the accurate reconstruction of any crime. And it is only the first step in a much broader forensic investigation, which includes autopsy and the careful laboratory analysis of evidence found at the scene. In the Dorothy Stratten case, it was immediately apparent that an intruder had not committed a double murder. Evidence pointed conclusively to murder followed by suicide. Yet a question remained when it was alleged that Dorothy Stratten was subjected to a sexual assault before her death.

Here again, forensic science provided the answer. Alert to that possibility, the investigator at the scene took fingernail scrapings and hair samples for analysis, and a sexual-assault test was performed. There were no laboratory findings of sexual abuse, only of "possible sexual activity." Thus, Dorothy Stratten's last moments of life before Paul Snider shot her in the head, then put the gun to his own head and pulled the trigger, must be left to conjecture.

AN "IMPOSSIBLE" DROWNING
The Case of Beach Boy Dennis Wilson

1

From the terrace of my small apartment in Marina del Rey, California, I could see the blue waters of the Pacific stretching toward the horizon. To my left, just across the street, one of the many picturesque marinas on this part of the coastline was crowded with boats of every kind from large luxurious yachts to tiny sailboats. In that very marina a few days before, on December 30, 1983, a Hollywood celebrity had met a very mysterious death. Dennis Wilson, a member of the legendary Beach Boys rock music group, had drowned in only twelve feet of water.

I felt a chill of recognition when I heard about the drowning, for the name Dennis Wilson was certainly familiar to me. In 1969, during my investigation of the murder of actress Sharon Tate and her friends by the Charles Manson "family," Wilson's name had turned up in a surprising fashion. It seemed that he had allowed the Manson cult to live in his house on Sunset Boulevard for a whole year, and had encouraged Manson as a musician. But then they had a falling out, Manson and his hippies had left—and Wilson told police he had received death threats.

Could his death be the culmination of one such threat? The autopsy had revealed bruises all over Wilson's face.

2

In 1961 Dennis Wilson rushed in from the beach to tell his brother Brian a wonderful idea for a song: the search for the perfect wave. Dennis and Brian, along with another brother, Carl, were then part of a rock group called Carl and the Passions, which also included a cousin, Mike Love, and a friend, Alan Jardine. Brian was the genius of the group; he took Dennis' idea and created a song that made rock-and-roll history: "Surfin'."

The song was an international hit, and the group soon changed its name to the Beach Boys, and added another musician, Bruce Johnston. They became the embodiment of California adolescent exuberance, their songs exuding the free spirit of the beach, fun in the sand, and pretty girls. But interestingly, only Dennis among the group was a surfer; the rest rarely saw the beach. And Brian, the writer who created such hits as "Surfin'," "Surf's Up," and "Surfin' Safari," was a moody recluse who spent most of his time indoors.

The Beach Boys surged to prominence in 1961 with a performance at Municipal Auditorium in Long Beach, California. Then they went on a national tour, and their music was embraced by young people everywhere. Their first million-selling album was "Good Vibrations," one of thirty-three albums they would eventually release. And in 1966 they were voted the world's most popular rock group in an English poll, supplanting the Beatles.

But in the late sixties, after the initial flood of surf and hot-rod hits had receded, their popularity began to decline and there was trouble within the group. Brian Wilson grew even more reclusive, hiding away from the others. Carl Wilson, the group's cohesive force, became embroiled with the government by resisting the draft as a conscientious objector. And Dennis Wilson, the free spirit, the one real surfer, lost himself in drugs and alcohol.

It was during that period that Dennis became involved with the Manson "family." And after they parted company, he was the target of several death threats, which he reported to police. But none of the threats ever materialized, and, as the years passed, Wilson told friends he thought this strange interlude in his life was at last behind him.

Meanwhile, his career was suffering. In fact, by 1982 the Beach Boys, beset with their internal problems, were lingering on the edge of oblivion. They were saved, ironically, by a man who denounced them, Secretary of the Interior James G. Watt. Even more ironically, Watt was right on target with his criticism—and yet he was the one who had to apologize.

Californians, headed by President Ronald Reagan, were in control of the Administration in Washington. What better group to perform for them at a July Fourth gala, they believed, than the quintessential Californians, the Beach Boys? Until Watt spoke up. He said the Beach Boys would attract "the wrong element" to the gala—and added, "We're not going to encourage drug abuse and alcoholism, as was done in years past."

Everyone, including President Reagan, sprang to the Beach Boys' defense, unaware that Dennis and Brian Wilson did have drug and alcohol problems. Nancy Reagan was quoted as saying to Watt, "I like the Beach Boys. My kids grew up with their music." In the end Watt had to apologize in public, showing reporters a large plaster foot with a hole in it to symbolize his having shot himself in the pedal extremity.

The publicity was sensational—and money in the bank. The Beach Boys were "hot" again. A show at LA's Universal Amphitheater after the Washington gala was a great success, and other dates followed. The only trouble was, Dennis was missing. Sadly, he was trying, and failing, to shake off his addiction to drugs and alcohol.

On Friday, December 23, 1983, Dennis checked into St. John's Hospital and Health Center in Santa Monica. He spoke at length to Dr. Jokichi Takamine, the doctor who would care for him at St. John's, about his desire to end his alcohol addiction. On December 24 they met again—but Christmas was the next day, a Sunday, and the doctor said he would be away. While he was gone on Christmas, Dennis checked out of the hospital.

3

On Tuesday, December 27, 1983, a man named Bill Oster was puttering about his boat, the *Emerald*, docked at a pier on Marquesas Way. The phone rang, and Oster heard the voice of an old friend, Dennis Wilson. Oster was glad to hear from him and agreed to pick up Wilson and a girl, Colleen "Crystal" McGovern.

Wilson, during a former marriage, had owned a boat, the *Harmony*, which he also kept at the Marquesas Way pier. He arrived on the *Emerald* with vodka and spent the rest of the day, and most of the night, drinking. Dennis told Oster about his proposed alcohol rehabilitation program, and added, "They won't let me back into the band until I do it." At about midnight he passed out, but an hour later he was up, and he spent a sleepless night, sometimes telephoning a former wife, Shaun, and former friends.

The next morning Colleen McGovern and Oster's fiancée, Brenda, hid the liquor from Dennis, while Oster suggested a healthy form of endeavor: rowing. But Dennis searched the boat until he found the hidden bottles and had a drink before going out rowing. They returned at noon, had turkey sandwiches, and somehow, by the end of lunch, Dennis had consumed three quarters of a fifth of vodka. Then, high on alcohol, he began diving into the slip next to the *Emerald*.

According to Oster, "He kept diving down, scrounging around, bringing up junk."

The water was a cold fifty-eight degrees. After twenty minutes of diving, Dennis was shivering, his teeth chattering.

So he took another drink, and started diving again.

It soon became apparent to Oster what "junk" Dennis was diving for. He was coming to the surface with objects that had once been on his own boat, one of them a silver frame that had held a picture of himself and Karen Camm, an ex-wife whom he had married twice.

Back on board, Dennis resumed his drinking, finishing the vodka and then starting on wine. Then he made one more dive. Oster, standing on the pier watching, believed he saw Dennis come up to within two feet of the surface, then swim behind the rowboat out of sight. He even thought he heard him take a breath of air.

Oster then said he saw Dennis go straight down and back out of sight. He waited for him to surface. Nothing happened. He remembered smoking a few cigarettes on the run on the pier, becoming more and more nervous as Dennis failed to reappear. Then a harbor patrol boat passed by and he hailed it.

In the words of Coroner's investigator Laverne Butler in her report:

> Decedent was observed by the patrol at the bottom of the pier, in twelve feet of water. He was placed on the dock at 1745 hours by Jim Hazelwood of the harbor patrol; death was pronounced at 1748 hours by Hazelwood.
>
> Mr. Oster states he and the decedent had been drinking alcohol since 1100 hours this date; he states the decedent was diving with a mask only, no snorkel. He watched the decedent dive into the water from the pier.
>
> Decedent was observed in a supine position on the dock. . . . He was not wearing a mask. He was clad in a pair of cut-off jeans, his left eye appeared blue, a small laceration on the bridge of his nose and his forehead.

Dr. J. Lawrence Cogan performed the autopsy on Wilson's body. In his report, he stated that there was a bruise in the forehead area:

> . . . a rectangular shaped area of abrasion and contusion. It measures 1 × 2 inches. It is associated with subcutaneous hemorrhage. The scalp beneath is free of fracture and there are no contusions of the brain noted. The skin about the area has a yellowish-greenish tinge. In the center of this area there is a small rectangular shaped abraded area measuring approximately ¼ inch. This appears recent. Over the left eye . . . are areas of contusion. They roughly cover an area of 2 × 3 inches. . . . There is noted a small superficial abrasion over the bridge of the nose measuring less than ¼ inch in greatest dimension.

Bruises were also found "over the left side of the face over the outer prominence, a small abrasion over the chin area, and a small amount of hemorrhage in the subcutaneous tissue in the left temporal muscle."

The near-impossibility of suddenly drowning in twelve feet of water, plus the bruises and the Manson connection, worried police. But their investigation revealed that two nights before the drowning Wilson had been involved in a barroom fight at the Santa Monica Bay Inn, and the bruises had most likely occurred there. As for the Manson connection, a murder underwater would have required a killer with a snorkel—too fanciful a concept to be considered seriously. But if the strange "accident" was not a murder, after all, what was the reason for drowning in such shallow water?

Because Los Angeles is situated along the ocean, I became very interested in underwater deaths early in my career as Chief Medical Examiner, and sponsored many studies of such tragedies. For that reason, I followed the newspaper accounts of Wilson's death closely. And when the toxicology report released on January 14, 1984, revealed that Wilson at the time of his death had a blood alcohol level of 0.26—more than twice the legal impairment limit for driving—I believe I found the scientific explanation of the probable cause of his drowning.

Underwater pressure causes nitrogen to be absorbed into the blood, which results in euphoria—that strange, carefree feeling familiar to all deep-sea divers due to nitrogen narcosis. The deeper you go, the graver the danger. Wilson went down only twelve feet, but unfortunately there was another biological factor in his system encouraging euphoria: alcohol. Therefore he stayed down much longer than he would have if he had been sober. He was poking around happily on the sea bed looking for objects from his former boat, unaware of his danger, when, suddenly, his breath ran out and he ingested water into his lungs. He couldn't make it back to the surface and safety.

The lesson of Dennis Wilson's death is clear: Stay out of the water if you have had anything at all to drink. Thus the man who created the first rock song about fun in the ocean, "Surfin'," may have served his ocean-loving fans one more time, not by music but by his own sad, and unnecessary, death.

PRESCRIPTION FOR DEATH
The Case of Elvis Presley

1

Elvis Presley was a phenomenon without equal in the entertainment world. He created and symbolized a musical style, rock and roll, in the fifties, which has lasted into the eighties. *New York Times* music critic John Rockwell wrote:

> For most people Elvis Presley was rock-and-roll. And they were right. Bill Haley may have made the first massive rock hit, and people such as Chuck Berry and Little Richard may have had an equally important creative impact on this raucous new American art form. But it was Elvis who defined the style and gave it an indelible image.

In his lifetime Presley sold over hundreds of millions of records—but there was more than music in his appeal. There was sex. When, early in his climb to fame, he appeared on *The Ed Sullivan Show* on CBS Television, he was photographed only from the waist up. CBS censors had decreed that America could not see the wildly gyrating hips that galvanized his young female fans at live concerts.

Elvis Presley had it all. Ruggedly handsome, with black hair cascading over his forehead, and eyes brooding as he swiveled, stomped and gyrated to pounding rhythms, he possessed a sex appeal that guaranteed success. But fate had given him yet another blessing: real musical talent.

That combination made him millions of dollars. He was idolized by his fans, and applauded by critics. He had his own private plane, dozens of luxurious cars (he gave Cadillacs as gifts to strangers) and a host of friends. But on August 16, 1977, it came to an end suddenly and prematurely. With sad irony, Elvis Presley's death at forty-two offered his adoring fans perhaps their first real glimpse into his frenetic lifestyle.

For one thing, Elvis and his fiancée, lovely Ginger Alden, twenty, had gone to the dentist at *midnight*. The reason for treatment at that strange hour was to avoid being mobbed by Elvis's fans, who were always on a vigil outside his house. Ginger had her teeth X-rayed; Elvis had a cavity filled.

When they returned to Graceland, the elaborate twenty-two-room mansion which Elvis had bought when the deluge of money began, they discussed plans for their upcoming wedding, deciding to make the announcement at Christmas. Then they went in to see Lisa Marie, Elvis's nine-year-old daughter born to his first wife, Priscilla, who had divorced him in 1973. Lisa Marie was there on a visit. By then it was 5 A.M., and what did Elvis want to do at that early hour in the morning? Play racquetball. He and Ginger roused two visiting cousins, and the four of them trooped outside and played racquetball on a lighted court until 7 A.M.

After the game Presley was still not sleepy. He dressed in a pair of blue pajamas and told Ginger he was "going to the bathroom to read a book."

Ginger went to sleep and, not surprisingly after the long night's activity, did not awaken until two the next afternoon. Elvis wasn't in bed. She went to the bathroom door and called his name. Later, she told a reporter for the Memphis *Commerical Appeal* what happened next.

> He didn't answer so I opened his bathroom door and that's when I saw him in there. I thought at first he might have hit his head because he had fallen . . . and his face was buried in the carpet. I slapped him a few times and it was like he breathed once when I turned his head. I raised one of his eyes and it was just blood red. But I couldn't move him.

She rushed out and called Elvis's bodyguards. The two men beat on Elvis's chest and tried mouth-to-mouth resuscitation, but it was too late.

The King of Rock and Roll was dead.

2

Elvis Presley was born in Tupelo, Mississippi, on January 8, 1935, the son of a poor farmer. When he was fourteen, the family moved to Memphis and lived in a public housing project. But his poverty-blighted childhood had one luminous aspect: music. His father, Vernon, and mother, Gladys, taught Elvis to sing, and the trio entertained at rural revivals and camp meetings in the area.

Elvis always had to help his parents pay the bills. Attending L. O. Humes High School, he worked as an usher at a movie theater, and after graduation he got a job as a truck driver for thirty-five dollars a week. At the wheel of the truck in 1953, he often passed the Sun Record Company, a recording studio. And one day he had an impulse (in his words, "just an urgin' ") that changed the world of American music forever. He turned off the road into the parking lot of the studio, went inside, and said he wanted to record a song. The owners said fine, but it would cost him one dollar.

The recorded song, Elvis said later, "sounded like somebody beating on a lid." But owner Sam Phillips was impressed with his voice, although he still remembered to take Elvis's dollar. Elvis thought that was the end of it. But Sam Phillips remembered the boy with the mellow voice who recorded his own song. He called Elvis and asked him if he could return to the studio to record a song, "Without You."

"Without You" was a ballad, and while Elvis was to break many young girls' hearts with his renditions of soulful ballads in the future, his first attempt was a failure. Phillips was disappointed, and told him to forget it. But after a coffee break, Elvis, on his own, started to sing a song with a rock-and-roll beat. Phillips and everyone else in the studio stood transfixed. They had never heard or seen anyone like the dynamic young man with a guitar pounding out a song.

Within days they recorded Elvis singing "That's All Right, Mama," and "I Don't Care If the Sun Don't Shine," and had them played on a local radio station, WHBG. The record sold seven thousand copies that first week in Memphis—and word filtered through the South to a man once described as a "country slicker," "Colonel" Thomas A. Parker, from Madison, Tennessee. Parker drove to Memphis and agreed to manage Elvis Presley.

Parker, a colorful figure sometimes seen in a ten-gallon hat, apparently was just the type of manager Presley needed, wise to the ways of the South and the appeal of a rawboned young guitarist. For living money, he first sent Elvis touring through the rural areas, billing him as "the Hillbilly Cat" in roadhouses deep in piney woods and very far from the big time. But all the while his records were reaching an ever larger audience. Then in 1956 came Elvis's first big hit, "Heartbreak Hotel," described as a "blood-stirring dirge about love and loneliness." It went "gold," selling more than two million records.

Elvis Presley was famous. Other hit records followed, and Elvis embarked on huge, sold-out concert tours and appeared in Las Vegas, Miami and other resort-area hotels and clubs. Then it was on to Hollywood and movie fame. The story of Parker's contract negotiation for Elvis's first motion picture role would become part of the Presley legend. The studio, 20th Century–Fox, said to the "country slicker," about the fee, "Would twenty-five thousand dollars be all right?" Colonel Parker replied, "That's fine for me. Now how about the boy?"

Presley would eventually star in dozens of films, each one a money-making hit. In 1966 there came a brief interruption in his career; the U.S. Army called. Presley, uncomplainingly and courteously, served his two years, ending up a sergeant in Germany. Returning to Memphis, he brought with him a fourteen-year-old girl, Priscilla Beaulieu, whom he had met in Europe. They lived at Graceland, soon married and had a child. But gold records, hit movies, sold-out performances were Elvis's life, and he was on the road almost constantly, living on the fast track night after night. It could not last. Perhaps inevitably, a new phenomenon had emerged in the midsixties, the Beatles, and Elvis's fame began to decline. Worse, he put on weight and began to look bloated. Somehow he still created electricity on stage and his records still sold millions, but in the 1970s he cut down on his appearances and concert tours, stopped making movies, and began spending more time at home.

Through it all, ups and downs, Elvis lost his wife but never lost his fanatical following. At forty-two, he could look forward to a long life in luxurious semi-retirement, but in 1977, seemingly robust, he suddenly died. Why? his fans clamored to know. The world press focused on the Chief Medical Examiner's Office in Memphis, and madness reigned throughout the modest-sized Southern city as tens of thousands of fans poured in to express their grief at the shrine of their idol.

3

On the day of Elvis's death I was in my office in the Forensic Science Center in Los Angeles, when my secretary buzzed me on the telephone. "It's Dr. Jerry Francisco from Memphis, Dr. Noguchi."

Driving to work that morning, I had heard over my car radio about Elvis Presley's death, and I knew that my friend Dr. Francisco, the Chief Medical Examiner of Shelby County, Tennessee, would be under extreme pressure. Indeed, that's what Jerry wanted to talk about.

"I know what you went through with the press when Senator Kennedy died out there," he said. "It's almost as bad down here now. I wanted your advice on how to handle the situation."

I told him that because the eyes of the world were on him, he should appoint a panel of distinguished pathologists to assist him with the autopsy. I had done that in the Kennedy autopsy, I said, and it had been useful in assuring the public that the autopsy would be properly performed. Jerry thanked me and, after he hung up, did exactly as I had suggested, appointing a panel of experts to assist at the autopsy. But unfortunately, the findings of that autopsy, instead of quelling public suspicion, aroused a heated controversy which endures to this day.

In a press conference conducted after the release of the official autopsy report, Francisco told reporters that Elvis Presley's death was due to "an erratic heartbeat. There was severe cardiovascular disease present." Francisco went on to say that Presley "had a history of mild hypertension and some coronary artery disease. These two diseases may be responsible for cardiac arrhythmia [irregular heartbeat] but the precise cause was not determined. Basically it was a natural death. The precise cause of death may never be discovered."

Rumors of a drug overdose involved in Presley's death were already circulating, and Francisco dismissed them with the statement that "there was no indication of any drug abuse of any kind." He said the only evidence of drugs involved those Presley was taking for his physical condition—mild hypertension and a colon problem.

That was, in fact, an understatement. For Presley had died with an almost unheard-of variety of drugs in his system. Among them were: (1) an antihistimine often used to control hayfever and allergies; (2) codeine, a derivative of opium used to relieve pain; (3) Demerol, a narcotic used as a sedative; (4) several tranquilizers, including Valium; (5) a sedative-hypnotic.

In sum, there were eight different drugs in his blood, but all were "harmless" *prescription* drugs. There was no trace of the illegal drugs such as heroin, cocaine or hashish normally found in overdose cases. Furthermore, not one of the prescription drugs was at a toxic level.

Nevertheless, the presence of all those drugs

shifted the spotlight from Francisco to the doctor who had prescribed them, because Presley's fans wanted to know whether their idol had somehow been "hooked" on drugs by an unscrupulous physician. Soon an official investigation of Presley's personal physician, George Nichopoulos, M.D., was begun, and the facts that investigation uncovered were startling—and dismaying to Presley's idolators.

The figures were staggering; indeed, incredible. In the seven months before Presley's death, Nichopoulos had prescribed 5300 stimulants, depressants and painkillers for Presley to take.

With this new evidence of drug use, Dr. Francisco had to call another press conference in 1979, this time to say, "I am not involved and never have been involved in a cover-up." And then he made good use of the panel that I had suggested he convene two years before. He said that three pathologists and one toxicologist from the University of Tennessee, and two other toxicologists from other areas, had agreed "there is no evidence the medication present in the body of Elvis Presley caused or made any significant contribution to his death."

A third toxicologist, Dr. Francisco said, had noted that the medications were in the therapeutic range and individually did not constitute an overdose. Also, he reemphasized the fact that the drugs were prescription; no illegal drugs had turned up in the autopsy.

By this time the American public was justifiably confused. Drug-overdose deaths were so common, from urban slums to the glittery palaces of Beverly Hills, that suspicion lingered about Presley's death. But how could prescription drugs that were not illegal, and not at toxic levels, have caused it?

That question was answered in September 1979,

when ABC-TV's "20/20" program televised a story
on the investigation of Dr. Nichopoulos. Featured was
my colleague Dr. Cyril Wecht, a hightly respected
pathologist, who is extremely articulate—and feisty,
to boot. In his vivid way, Wecht explained that prescription drugs at nontoxic levels still can kill. Elvis
Presley, he said, "was a walking drugstore." His death
was caused by a condition pathologists call "polypharmacy." In this condition, it is not the individual drugs
that kill, but their reaction with each other to form a
fatal combination. "The combined effects of eight different drugs in Presley's body at the time of death was
to depress first the brain and then the heart and
lungs," Wecht said. However, he went on to say that
he believed Presley's death was accidental "with the
patient not realizing what the effect would be."

Anger boiled over at Dr. Nichopoulos. One de-
ranged Presley fan even fired a rifle at him when he
attended a baseball game, and police had to place the
physician under a round-the-clock guard to protect his
life. Then in 1980, Dr. Nichopoulos went before the
Tennessee Board of Medical Examiners on charges of
misconduct in his treatment of the singer. Silver-
haired, his diamond rings flashing in the light from
the ceiling, the physician admitted that Elvis gobbled
drugs "from the time he woke up in the morning until
the time he went to sleep at night."

Nichopoulos said Presley was a "psychological" addict who had been treated in hospitals in 1973 and
1974 for detoxification from Demerol, a painkiller,
and other drugs. Then he went on to give an insight
into the famous singer's life on the road. Dr. Nichopoulos always went along, he said, carrying three suit-
cases filled with drugs for Presley and his retinue.
When a concert was scheduled, Nichopoulos, the

week before, would prescribe a "protocol," a program of strong doses of amphetamines, depressants and painkillers. Presley had died during one of those protocols, which involved 680 pills and 20 cubic centimeters of liquid downers, uppers and painkillers.

But Nichopoulos also presented persuasive evidence that he had sought to control Presley's drug habits, often substituting placebos for the prescribed drugs. Whenever he did that, however, Presley obtained his drugs from other sources. The jury believed Nichopoulos could not control Presley and declared the doctor innocent.

4

January 8, 1985, would have been the late Elvis Presley's fiftieth birthday, and Memphis, Tennessee, was once again the center of the music world. Thousands of Presley fans descended on the city, flocking through Graceland, which had been turned into a museum, and laying flowers on his grave, many in bouquets shaped like guitars. That same day Memphis officials announced plans to build a memorial fountain and park across the street from the mansion dedicated to the memory of their most famous citizen.

That night I watched a televised concert of Elvis Presley which was being shown as part of the nationwide celebration of his birthday. There he was, handsome, muscular, strumming a guitar with an electric driving rhythm, and I thought back once more to his death. Just recently I had spoken to Dr. Francisco's associate, James Spencer Bell, at a medical convention in San Antonio, Texas. Bell was there with some other Memphis pathologists, and they were bombarded with questions about Presley. He said that Jerry Francisco, despite the criticism, was still absolutely convinced that Presley did *not* die of drugs. But Bell refused to give any reasons for Francisco's stand other than what was publicly known, because he was under court order not to discuss the controversial autopsy.

But later another Memphis pathologist told me that Presley had been able to function normally to the end, which is not the case in polypharmacy victims, who are dazed and drowsy when near death and almost unable to move. Specifically, Presley had gone to the bathroom and had started washing and preparing for bed. In the midst of those preparations, his heart had suddenly given way, and he toppled over, dead of a heart attack. The ability to function normally until the end was the reason that Dr. Francisco believed Presley did not die from polypharmacy.

But even if that is true, and Presley did die of a heart attack, the root cause of his death, in my opinion, was the combination of prescription drugs he ingested in such quantities that it caused the fatally irregular heartbeat in the first place.

One of my maxims as a forensic scientist has alwyas been "We learn from the dead." The facts and circumstances of a death can assist those who are living to prevent similar needless tragedies. For that reason, Elvis Presley's death should raise a red flag for Americans, and people around the world. Many, many people take prescription drugs in combination, perhaps a tranquilizer and an antihistamine, codeine and aspirin, or others even more dangerous. The lesson from the Presley case is clear: Seemingly safe prescription drugs can be as fatal as illegal drugs if taken in combination. Persons ingesting more than one drug should monitor themselves very carefully, in cooperation with a physician.

Elvis Presley's first hit was "Heartbreak Hotel." When his own heart "broke," a lot of joy vanished from the world. But it is my hope that his untimely death will lead to some good in its wake, alerting people to the danger of "safe" prescription drugs that can kill in combination.

THE "DETECTIVE OF DEATH"

A coroner whose jurisdiction includes Hollywood will find himself involved in world-famous cases throughout his career. The death of a celebrity inevitably attracts the attention of both the press and the public. But as a medical examiner I often noted a surprising phenomenon. Reporters and journalists who came to call on me appeared to be equally fascinated by the puzzling twists of the *little-known* forensic cases I had investigated. I became something of a celebrity myself—to my surprise and later regret—as reporters began to refer to me as "the Detective of Death." A sort of Sherlock Holmes legend was created about me, a legend which culminated in the production of the popular television series, *Quincy*, supposedly based on my exploits.

In fact there is nothing mysterious or magical about the work of a forensic detective. On rare occasions I have had a flash of insight that led me to the resolution of a case. But even then, as with every other case, the resolution came only after very careful investigation, and was supported by irrefutable forensic facts.

I have often wondered how Sherlock Holmes or any

of the many other detectives of fiction would fare as a medical examiner of a large city. There are no dramatic chases, no physical confrontations with cunning criminals. The work, for the most part, is hard and routine, without the glamour and excitement of fictional thrillers. Nevertheless, I have been confronted with cases that might confound the deductive powers of even the great Sherlock Holmes. Truth, in my experience, is always stranger than fiction.

THE MISSING BABY

A mother hysterically called the Los Angeles Police Department to say that her baby was missing. Police went to the home and scoured the grounds, including the swimming pool. When the baby was not found, they suspected a kidnapping. Newspapers printed the story, and for three weeks this case gripped Los Angeles as the anxious parents and the police waited for word from the kidnappers. No word came.

Then one day a torrential rain struck Los Angeles. When the downpour ended, the mother happened to glance out of the kitchen window—and saw her baby floating face down in the swimming pool, dead.

It was a mystery. The police had searched the pool at the time the baby was reported missing and had not seen it. They speculated that a kidnapper had murdered the baby, or it had died while in his keeping, and he had returned to the house and thrown it into the pool.

I performed the autopsy. Forensic clues immediately told me that the baby had been alive when drowned, not murdered beforehand as everyone thought. There was fluid in its lungs which had been inhaled. Also, the baby had what housewives call "dishwater hands"—a wrinkling of the skin caused by moisture which affects blood circulation. Dead bodies have no blood circulation and therefore no "dishwater hands." This fact also meant the baby had been alive when it went into the pool.

Had the baby been taken back to the pool alive and thrown in? Unlikely as that seemed, there was forensic evidence to back it. I did not think the body was as decomposed as it should have been if it had been submerged for three weeks. But then I noticed another forensic clue—little green clusters on the baby's white pullover sweatshirt. I called an oceanographic expert, who analyzed the clusters and found that they were algae, underwater organisms that grow on objects. The extent of the growth on the baby's shirt would have taken twenty days, almost exactly the length of time the baby had been missing. To me, that was definite proof that the baby had been submerged for three weeks. I noticed further that once the baby's body had been exposed to air, it then began to decompose at an abnormally rapid rate, another sign that death had occurred weeks before.

All the evidence now pointed to an accidental drowning. But one troublesome question remained: why had no one discovered the body? I sent an investigator to look at the pool, and we had the answer. The investigator reported that the water in the pool was not clear but murky. Because the police had searched, but not drained, the pool at the time of the baby's disappearance, they had missed the body. Nor had the mother seen it in her search. Only after torrential rains had stirred up the water in the pool did the body finally rise to the surface.

ALL IN THE SAME BOAT

On a sunny day in the waters off Santa Barbara, a man was rowing a dory from his sailboat toward shore with his wife, his small stepson and their pet dog, enjoying the spectacular views from the sea of cliffside homes and the mountains rising in the distance.

Then, out of sight of the shore, something happened. The man returned to the dock alone with a terrible story to tell. The dog had jumped out of the boat. His little stepson had tried to rescue it and capsized the boat. Both the wife and the boy had been struck by the sharp edges of the craft and had drowned, despite his efforts to save them.

The police who investigated the tragedy were suspicious. But there were no witnesses, and, seemingly, no possible clues. The incident had taken place out at sea, with no other boats in sight. Was it an accident —or the perfect crime? There seemed to be no answer to that question. Furthermore, the suspect, an experienced sailor, was able to fortify his story with data such as the precise momentum of the boat when it capsized, the angle at which it struck the victims, the velocity of the ocean current when he attempted to rescue his wife and stepson, and so forth.

What he didn't know was forensic pathology.

Every bruise is as individual as a fingerprint. In a crude way, you can create a library of bruise patterns right in your own home. Each sharp edge of a table, a desk or a chair can be catalogued. You simply take a sheet of carbon paper, place it between two blank white sheets, and bang the carbon sandwich sharply against the object.

When I was asked to assist in the investigation of this alleged "perfect crime," I was immediately interested in the bruises incurred by the victims. My first step was to visit the Coast Guard commander in Santa Barbara who had brought in the bodies. He informed me that the ocean was "stable" on the day of the accident, and it was unlikely that you could capsize such a boat in a calm sea by reaching overboard for a dog.

We found the boat sitting in a drydock, where it had been impounded by police. My request to the commander brought an arched eyebrow. "Could I borrow it for the weekend?"

"You want to take her out on the ocean?"

"Far from it. I want the boat delivered to my apartment in Los Angeles."

"Your *apartment?*"

"Right."

The commander was mystified, but within a few days I had a new piece of furniture in my living room, a boat that seemed as large as a battleship in that space.

Meanwhile, I had obtained magnified photographs

of the bruises incurred by the wife and the stepson. The son's wounds were on the back of the head, low on the skull. The wife's were on the top. My next step was to obtain mannequins that automobile manufacturers employ in their experiments with car crashes to analyze the strength of their vehicles. I borrowed two of these mannequins, one the size of the small boy, the other that of the woman. Then I began testing.

The wife was easy. On her mannequin, I affixed carbon duplicating paper over the area of the head where her bruise had been located. Then I placed the mannequin sitting upright on a seat in the boat. And finally, to test my theory of murder, I picked up the oar that had been in the boat and struck the mannequin over the head sharply from behind.

A pattern emerged on the duplicating paper. It was identical, when magnified, to the bruise pattern on the wife's skull.

The case of the little boy was more difficult. He had two bruises, both in an odd place, low on the back of his head. You don't normally strike someone there. And then I realized, chillingly, what had happened if my theory was correct. The man had disposed of his wife with the oar, but he didn't need such a weapon to murder the helpless little boy. He had taken his stepson by the ankles, held him upside down, and smashed his head against some hard object.

I made at least two dozen experiments in vain before I found that hard object—a steel seat support on the right side of the boat. The identical bruise patterns emerged when the little mannequin's head was swung and struck that enforcing bar.

Meanwhile, police had discovered a number of suspicious facts about the man. His previous wife had been found dead, mysteriously floating face down in

a hot tub at their home. Further, he had recently purchased a $400,000 life insurance policy on his new
wife, plus another $300,000 if death was caused by an
accident. It was also alleged that he had collected
large insurance payments on suspicious fires that
damaged his houseboat and a car.

This evidence, plus the forensic evidence of the
origin of the bruises found on the bodies of his wife
and his young stepson, resulted in the conviction of
the man for murder. And on May 5, 1985, Stanley M.
Roden, who was the prosecutor in the case, informed
me that an appeal of that conviction had recently been
denied.

THE "ACCIDENTAL" LOVER

A young man was found lying flat on his bed, blood
oozing from his temple, a .32 pistol on the floor. Soot
around the wound indicated that the bullet had been
fired from less than three inches away. The revolver
bore his fingerprints on its butt. An obvious suicide.
Or was it?

The young man's friends said he had been happy
before he died, and had no reason to commit suicide.
Could it have been murder? we wondered. On rare
occasions a killer arranges a murder to appear to be a
suicide, wiping off his own fingerprints from the gun

and applying the victim's fingerprints on its butt. But there again we were stopped, as friends said the young man had no enemies of any kind and was not into drugs or other illegal activities.

Still I was concerned. Why would a healthy, happy young man commit suicide? With some misgivings, we issued a judgment of suicide. But then I received a telephone call from the victim's young wife, and one of the strangest inquests in my experience resulted. She demanded a public hearing on the cause of death, claiming that it had not been suicide or murder—it was an accident.

When the inquest was convened, the pretty young wife took the stand and testified that she and her husband had been making love when the gun was fired. To say the least, her testimony claimed the attention of the court. She then said her husband had sexual problems. He could not fulfill his function as a lover unless he pointed a loaded gun at his head.

Perilous, but efficient. They had successfully achieved intercourse many times in this fashion, but on the fatal night, in a convulsive seizure of passion, he had accidentally pulled the trigger.

The hearing officer, in one of the most bizarre coroner's cases in Los Angeles history, believed the wife and ruled the young man's death accidental.

And we had to amend the death certificate.

THE FUNHOUSE CORPSE

In April 1981 my secretary sent the following letter to Frederick Olds, the director of the Oklahoma Territorial Museum in Guthrie, Oklahoma.

DEAR MR. OLDS:

Hope this helps. I measured Dr. Noguchi's head and the results were 26¾".

He has a Stetson Western hat size 7 which is a little tight, and a soft hat, size 7, which is a fairly good fit.

If the above is not sufficient, please let me know.

RITA

This discussion of my hat size had a unique beginning in a "house of horrors," paradoxically called by its owners a "funhouse."

In 1976 the producers of the popular television series "The Six Million Dollar Man" decided to stage a suspenseful sequence at the Nu-Pike Funhouse in Long Beach, California, part of a large amusement park. The funhouse was one of the park's main attractions. In its eerie confines, skeletons sprang from closets, ghosts appeared suddenly in white sheets, and gruesome props of all kinds terrorized the visitors who happily paid for the privilege of risking death by heart attack.

The television crewmen who moved in to prepare for the production of "The Six Million Dollar Man" were delighted by these props which would add such color to their show. They particularly liked one of the dummies because it was so unusual. It was a "cowboy," painted a neon orange, which hung gruesomely from a gallows by a rope. The sign under it said "Oklahoma Badman." The director decided definitely to use that one, and ordered his crewmen to move it to a location where the film's action would take place.

Probably no fictional thrill on the television series ever equaled the real shock the crew experienced next. While they were moving the painted dummy, its arm suddenly broke off—*and a human bone was revealed!* Quickly the police were called, and then the coroner's office. The owners of the amusement park said they had no idea the dummy was human.

The newspapers had a lot of fun with the story of the prop that turned out to be a real corpse. Nevertheless, we at the coroner's office had to fulfill our function to investigate an unexplained death. And it was a case unique in our experience, because the body was not only long dead, but mummified. So how to identify him?

Our investigator who went to the scene obviously had some difficulty with his report on this particular victim. The report began well enough: "Body found hanging in funhouse at Nu-Pike Amusement Park, Long Beach, mummified." But almost all the items on the investigator's checklist, such as "birthplace," "name and birthplace of father," "street address," etc., had to be marked "unknown." "Sex" was marked "M" but "color or race" received a "?" Weight of the corpse was estimated at only fifty pounds, and height at sixty-three inches. I particularly liked the investigator's response to the question of the body's condition: "Fair, mummified."

Dr. Joseph Choi, one of my best pathologists, performed the autopsy on the mummified corpse. He found that all of the body's major internal organs, from the heart to the liver, were present, although "hard as a rock" from arsenic embalming. In addition, he found that the unknown man had been killed by a "gunshot wound through the chest to the abdomen." And furthermore, Dr. Choi recovered the copper jacket of the bullet that had killed him from "the muscle of the left pelvic area."

It was about then I heard from Fred Olds, whose Oklahoma Territorial Museum celebrates the badmen in the state's past as part of its colorful Wild West heritage. Olds wondered if the corpse could be that of Elmer J. McCurdy, a notorious railroad bandit who had been killed in a gunfight with an Oklahoma sheriff's posse in 1911.

"Tell me why you think it's McCurdy," I said, and Olds described the colorful story of McCurdy's life and death.

"He was a hard drinker and a loner," he said. "He robbed trains, cracked safes and used his six-shooter to kill a man in Colorado."

But McCurdy never had much luck as a lawbreaker, Olds told me. For instance, he always seemed to hold up the wrong train. In 1911 he was waiting for a train carrying several thousand dollars to be paid to the Osage Indians. But, as usual, the train he robbed was the wrong one, just ahead of the money train. All he got for his trouble was $46 cash, two jugs of whiskey —and a sheriff's posse hot on his trail.

The posse tracked McCurdy to a barn. There he fought it out in true Wild West style, sniping at the sheriff's men while they pegged bullets at him from every direction. Finally the shooting ended, and the lawmen found McCurdy dead. But he was to prove just as unlucky in death as he had been in life. He was

taken to nearby Pawhuska and embalmed with arsenic in a funeral home. But no relatives ever showed
up to claim the body.

In those days it was common practice for the mummified bodies of famous badmen like Jesse James and
the Dalton Brothers to be exhibited in carnival side-
shows that toured the country. To their credit, the
mortuary owners refused all such offers for McCurdy
—until four years later when two "cousins" from California showed up and said they wanted to give their
relative a decent burial in California.

The fraudulent cousins then proceeded to exhibit
McCurdy for years until his notoriety was exhausted
and the body vanished from sight, stored in a ware-
house with dummies. Later some of these dummies
were sent off to an amusement park, and apparently
McCurdy's body accidentally went with them, eventually ending up in the gallows display as a prop. Or
so Olds believed. But how could we prove the body
really was McCurdy's?

Oddly, McCurdy had never been fingerprinted, but
Olds said he had a set of documents and photographs
that could be helpful. When the railroad bandit had
been embalmed in 1911, his body had been not only
measured by the mortuary, but photographed for record collection purposes.

I thought, Shades of Alphonse Bertillon, who decades ago invented anthropometry, the photographing
and measuring of criminals as a means of later identification. Years after anthropometry had fallen into disfavor I would be using it again—but with modern
techniques too. In fact, McCurdy could be a test case
for an identification technique I had been thinking of
which I called "medial superimposition."

I ordered radiographs taken of McCurdy's head and

superimposed them on the 1911 photographs of McCurdy's face. I then superimposed the negatives of the 1911 photos on the actual head. The bone configurations matched identically in both comparisons, and the measurements of the body did, too. For while bodies "shrink" in death, the bones remain the same, and provide measurements of the body's height, as well as the length of arms and legs.

The final clue was also derived from the documents made by that funeral home decades ago. A scar was said to be present on McCurdy's right wrist. This scar was not easy to find under coats of paint, but we did so, and the identification was complete.

And so, finally, the "Oklahoma Badman" arrived home, and at last had some luck. In an impressive funeral attended by newspaper and television reporters from all over the Southwest, McCurdy was grandly buried in "Boot Hill," the territorial section of the Guthrie cemetery, close by the graves of the Bill Doolin Gang and other desperados of those frontier days. In one of the great understatements of the day, Ralph McCalmont, representing the city of Guthrie, told reporters at the cemetery, "He probably would have been buried here anyway, but he got *sidetracked.*"

Sometime later I found myself riding in an old fire engine in a parade during the annual '89-er Celebration in Guthrie. Because of my successful efforts in identifying the railroad bandit, I had been invited to the celebration as a special guest. In fact, as soon as I arrived at the airport, I was taken to a "cowboy shop" and fitted with the black hat, black boots and cowboy costume of a frontier doctor, which I wore proudly.

As I rode along in the parade, I marveled again at

the wonders of America, whose citizens delighted so much in their colorful past, including their gun-toting Wild West bandits, and most particularly, on that day, Elmer J. McCurdy, the funhouse corpse.

FORENSIC PUZZLES OF THE PAST

Forensic scientists are, by nature, extremely inquisitive, and every year we travel to cities across America and around the world to attend conferences and seminars on various fields of interest to our profession. Many of us belong to a variety of organizations, such as the International Association of Forensic Science, the World Association of Medical Law (of which I am currently vice-president), the National Academy of Forensic Science, and the National Association of Medical Examiners. We meet together often, as professionals and as friends. To laymen, a convention of coroners might appear to be a rather morbid group. But, in fact, our meetings are lively occasions with much humor and banter, and energetic but good-willed debates on many subjects.

Because crimes and mysterious deaths have occurred for centuries, while forensic science is a relatively new field, we have much to debate. A hundred years after the events that made a certain killer famous, for example, we're still intrigued about the identity of Jack the Ripper. Other historical questions are equally fascinating to us. Did General Custer and his troops commit mass suicide? Was Napoleon murdered while in exile? Did Adolf Hitler, the archvillain of our century, escape from Berlin in the last days of the war? These are some of the classic historical mysteries which forensic scientists still investigate with often surprising results.

CUSTER'S LAST STAND

In 1984 archaeologists armed with metal detectors descended on the legendary site of "Custer's Last Stand." There, in the Battle of Little Big Horn in Montana on June 25, 1876, General George Armstrong Custer and 209 troopers of the Seventh Cavalry were surrounded and slaughtered by thousands of Indians on a grassy hilltop above the Little Big Horn River. Paintings of that battle ever since have shown the golden-haired General firing his pistol at the Indian warriors who whirled by on horses, fighting to the end.

Not for decades was this historical version of the battle challenged. A professor, Dr. Thomas B. Marquis, who in the 1920s wrote a book, *Keep the Last Bullet for Yourself*, disputing that heroic version of the battle, could not obtain a publisher. Incredibly, it was not until 1976, forty-one years after Dr. Marquis died, that his work was published.

Marquis had been a physician assigned to the Cheyenne Indian Reservation in the early years of this century. Survivors of the battle were still alive, and what they told Marquis stunned him. There had been no hilltop battle as described at all. Custer and his troopers were surrounded, but no Indians had charged either on horse or on foot. Instead they had dismounted and hidden in gullies and draws on the hillside, merely sniping at the soldiers on the ridge with a few guns, or launching arrows toward the hill from below.

Earlier a brave detachment of troopers, few in number, had charged down the hill, attempting to break out of the encirclement, and they had been killed. But the approximately two hundred soldiers on the hilltop were still in fortified positions, and the Indians knew that a frontal attack would be foolhardy. So they waited for dark, but suddenly, to their astonishment, there was a flurry of gunfire on the hill above them. Then silence. An Indian scout crawled up the hill under cover of the bushes and saw an incredible scene. Custer and his men all lay dead.

So went Dr. Marquis's tale, as learned from the Indians, a version of the battle outrageous to American patriots. For some of the soldiers had been killed by snipers, according to Marquis, but Custer and the bulk of his troops had committed mass suicide rather than suffer torture at the hands of the Indians.

Outrageous—but there were some facts that appeared to back up the story. For example, only about a dozen Indians died in the battle, as against the more than two hundred American soldiers who perished. Also, very few expended shells were found on the hilltop, indicating that not much firing had been done by the soldiers.

In 1982 Navy Commander Jerry Spencer, formerly of the Armed Forces Institute of Pathology, presented the mass suicide theory at a conference of the American Academy of Forensic Sciences. He said that he had requested exhumation of the skeletons for examination. His presentation, reprinted in *The Journal of Forensic Sciences*, explained why.

With the techniques of modern forensic science, it would be possible to substantiate the suicide theory of Dr. Marquis if the skeletons could be examined.

Most individuals who commit suicide with a firearm shoot themselves in the head, with the muzzle of the weapon in contact or loose contact with the head. Besides the bullet, a large quantity of powder residue is driven into the scalp tissue and into the skull, where it will remain indefinitely.

Sophisticated techniques such as scanning electron microscopy with X-ray diffraction analysis could be used to evaluate the skulls for powder residue. Because of the type of gunpowder used in 1876, however, these techniques would be unnecessary. At that time "black powder," a mixture of charcoal, sulfur and potassium nitrate, was used as the propellant in both rifle and handgun bullets, rather than the modern "smokeless" gunpowder, or nitrocellulose. Black powder in ignition produces very large quantities of powder residue, much more than smokeless powder.

Presumably, if most of the skulls revealed evidence of black-powder residue, we would have proof of one of the greatest disgraces in American history, mass suicide in front of the enemy. But permission to exhume the skeletons had been refused by the superintendent of the Custer monument.

Forensic scientists, like most Americans, are fascinated by Custer's Last Stand. I remember that once, during a coffee break in a National Medical Examiners meeting in Newport, California, a young female reporter for the Los Angeles *Times* approached me and asked a different type of question from those I usually hear: "Dr. Noguchi, what do coroners talk about at cocktail parties?"

I'm afraid I made her laugh when I replied, "Well, last night we spent the whole evening arguing whether General Custer committed suicide."

My friend Bill Eckert of Wichita, Kansas, is one of my colleagues most interested in Custer. Because of him I looked into the baffling mystery of the dead troopers myself. And my attention first centered on a second forensic enigma in that battle: the body of General Custer.

After the soldiers had died, the Indians stripped them of their uniforms and then proceeded to mutilate all the bodies in terrible fashion, chopping off legs, arms and heads, and scalping each and every man. Except General Custer. Alone among the mutilated bodies, he was untouched, though naked. A bullet was in his side, and one in his head.

There were many witnesses to this fact, because the reserve troops who came to the hill after the Indians had fled all gathered around the fallen General. But their testimony reveals forensic evidence which seems to refute Dr. Marquis's thesis, at least in Custer's case. The bullet hole in Custer's side was bloody; the hole in the head showed little blood. That means the shot that actually killed Custer struck him in the side, not a location which persons use to commit suicide by gun. The bullet in the head was probably a *coup de grâce* shot fired by an Indian after Custer was dead.

Why was Custer's body, alone, untouched and un-mutilated? Most Americans over the years have tended to believe it was because the Indians re-spected their greatest enemy. Not so, it seems. Custer had fought Indians in the Midwest; this was his first campaign in the North. The Northern Indians in the area had never heard of him, as almost all of them told interviewers over the years.

There was, however, one Indian chief, with the po-etic name Rain-in-the-Face, who *had* fought Custer before. Perhaps he intervened and saved Custer's body, and his dignity, for history. But an even more romantic idea emerged when historians discovered that a young Indian woman who had been a mistress of General Custer's was in the Cheyenne Indian vil-lage from which the warriors rode to battle. Perhaps she, among the squaws on the hill after the battle, protected Custer's body.

My own opinion on the controversy about Custer's Last Stand is that Custer was a brave man, as he had proved many times in the past. He would never have committed suicide. The forensic evidence of his two bullet wounds shows he was killed by a shot in the side.

I believe that Custer died early in the battle, no doubt astride his horse, showing his bravery to rally the spirit of the troops, when a sniper's bullet struck him in the side and killed him. Unfortunately, his best junior officers had been assigned to other regiments, and I believe the leaderless troops may have panicked with thousands of Indians surrounding them. That, in my opinion, is why so few shots were fired, and so few Indians died.

All of the troopers knew that Indians tortured sol-diers while they were alive, and perhaps some did commit suicide when all was known to be lost. But most, I'm sure, fought heroically to the end.

An archaeological dig in 1984 at the site of the Battle of Little Big Horn turned up some shells, and a finger bone encircled by a ring. But to date no more clues have been found to the mystery of Custer's Last Stand, that savage day on a hill when a few hundred Americans looked out at thousands of hostile Indians on every side—and wondered what to do.

THE DEATH OF NAPOLEON

1

St. Helena is a speck of land in the Atlantic Ocean which lies 1,750 miles from South Africa, 1,800 miles from South America, and, most important to the British, 4,000 miles from England. For there in exile in 1815 was Napoleon Bonaparte, England's hated rival, whose great armies had ruled Europe for years.

Exiled once before on an island closer to land, Napoleon had escaped, raised an army, and again terrorized Europe. In one of history's landmark battles, he was defeated by the Duke of Wellington at Waterloo, and this time the English took no chances. St. Helena was about as far from civilization as one could go, a rather pretty little island, green and hilly, but suffering from a terrible climate in which excessively hot spells alternated with blustery periods when an icy wind bent trees to the ground and tore through the thin wooden walls of the island dwellings.

There the exiled Emperor arrived on October 17, 1815, with a retinue of faithful servants and three former officers of his army, Count Charles-Tristan de Montholon, General Henri-Gratien Bertrand, and Count Emmanuel de Las Cases. Such was the devotion that Napoleon inspired that these three voluntarily chose to spend years in exile on this "godforsaken" island to be close to their imprisoned leader.

A garrison of three thousand British troops (on an island only six and a half miles wide and ten and a half miles long) was assigned to make certain Napoleon stayed a prisoner. Under the almost paranoiac supervision of Governor Hudson Lowe, they watched Napoleon's every move, and Lowe constantly kept placing new, and petty, restrictions on his dangerous captive.

By 1821, Napoleon was ill, and no one knew why. He was only fifty-one years old; he was not losing weight—indeed, he had *gained* poundage. And yet he complained of weakness and swelling of the ankles. On the fifth of May of that year he was dead. And not until his will was read was it discovered that, two months before he died, he had written the following words: "I am dying before my time, murdered by the English oligarchy *and its hired assassin.*"

The autopsy on his body was conducted with the ex-Emperor stretched naked on a billiard table in the house, Longwood, where he had died. Thereafter physicians reported a large benign ulcer in his stomach and an enlarged liver. Neither was the cause of death, although the discovery of the ulcer led people to believe that Napoleon died of cancer. The terrible words included in his will suggested another cause of death—murder.

But how had murder been done? Poison had not been found in Napoleon's stomach during the autopsy, and no violence had occurred. In fact, during his illness Napoleon was constantly attended closely by his fanatical followers.

The answer might never have been known had not Napoleon's loyal valet, Louis Marchand, shaved off his leader's hair in order to present locks of it to members of Napoleon's family and friends from the old days. Those locks of hair were preserved, and, 150 years later, one thin strand of that hair presented, through modern forensic science, a solution to the mystery.

2

Sten Forshufvud, a tall, lean blond Swede, was a Napoleon idolater whose house in Göteborg was filled with portraits, busts and statues of the Emperor. In 1955 Forshufvud read the memoirs of Louis Marchand, which recounted in diary fashion Napoleon's last days. According to Marchand, the diminutive Emperor, in his illness, had alternated between drowsiness and insomnia, his feet had become swollen, and he had been so weak that he complained, "My legs don't hold me up." Then during his very last days Napoleon had been administered tartar emetic and calomel, a "heroic" (10 gram) dose of the latter bringing on the final fainting and death.

The sequence leading to death constituted a pattern, Forshufvud realized upon reading Marchand's diary: slow poisoning by arsenic. The symptoms of such poisoning were all there: alternating somnolence and insomnia, swollen feet, general fatigue, and an enlarged liver. Because arsenic, Forshufvud believed, had been given to Napoleon in small doses over a long period of time, the poison had not been suspected. And the ingestion of tartar emetic and calomel in his last days had made it untraceable in the stomach.

From his studies, Forshufvud knew that arsenic has a special property. It is indestructible. If Napoleon's body could be examined, he could test it for arsenic traces. But the Emperor was buried in state in Paris, in a shrine visited by millions of tourists each year. Forshufvud realized he would never have a chance to prove his theory. But then he heard about the locks of hair. He traced a descendant of one of Napoleon's retinue on St. Helena, and obtained a strand of it for testing.

3

The investigation of the mystery of Napoleon's death is a textbook example of modern forensic technology at work. By 1962 scientists had developed equipment which bombarded an object with radiation to determine its elements. Forshufvud sent a strand of the hair he had obtained to a forensic scientist, Hamilton Smith, in Glasgow. In Smith's laboratory, the Scotsman weighed the lone hair strand and sealed it in a polyethylene container. Then the hair strand and a standard arsenic solution were both irradiated for twenty-four hours. The hair strand, it was discovered, contained 10.38 micrograms of arsenic per gram of hair, almost thirteen times the normal amount, which is 0.8 parts per million.

Excited by this discovery, Forshufvud traveled to Glasgow to confer with Smith. Nonbelievers, Forshufvud said, might declare that the arsenic could have come externally, in some way, from the natural environment, and not been ingested as a poison. Was there a method to discover if the arsenic had been taken internally?

Smith smiled. A few months earlier, he said, that would have been impossible, because his irradiation equipment did not have the capability of analyzing different *sections* of a hair strand—only the total strand. But he had just installed an improved technological device which could do so.

Why was *section* analysis important? Forshufvud asked, and Smith told him, "If arsenic was absorbed from the natural environment, the analyses of the hair strand would show a *constant* amount of arsenic along its length. If, on the other hand, arsenic was ingested into the body at intervals, the hair strand would show *peaks and valleys* of arsenic in each section." Furthermore, because hair grows at about .014 inches per day, Smith could calculate the time between the peaks.

Smith performed 140 tests on a new sample of hair which Forshufvud obtained from a lock that had been owned by one of Napoleon's valets, Jean-Abraham Noverraz. The section analyses showed that the arsenic had not come from the environment, because its content was not constant. Instead, it ranged from a low of 1.86 to a high of 51.2.

Forshufvud and Smith published their findings in the British scientific journal *Nature*, on October 14, 1961. Here, it appeared, was proof that the Emperor Napoleon had been assassinated, and the world was fascinated by the forensic detective work which had used modern devices to solve a murder more than a century and a half old.

But in academia a reaction always inspires a counter-reaction, and some scientists set out to disprove Forshufvud and Smith's theory. These scientists believed that the arsenic had entered Napoleon's hair naturally from the environment, and in the late seventies they had a find equal in significance to Forshufvud and Smith's analyses of Napoleon's hair. It was, believe it or not, Napoleon's wallpaper.

The culmination of their efforts, in which they exposed the wallpaper to neutron-activating equipment, was published in *Nature* magazine in 1982. *The New York Times,* with some amusement, wrote an editorial on the scientific debate, entitled "Arsenic and Old Napoleon":

> Two British scientists note that the emerald greens in 19th century wallpaper were made from a copper-arsenic pigment, which could be converted by a fungus into a deadly arsenical vapor. Having discovered scraps of Napoleon's St. Helena wallpaper in an old family scrapbook, they say it contains enough arsenic to cause illness, but not death. "Conspiracy theories need not be invoked to explain arsenic found in the hair," they conclude with a touch of scorn.

The *Times* went on to say that the original advocate of the poisoning theory, Sten Forshufvud, not only hotly contested the British scientists' findings, but thought their theory was "off the wall."

Napoleon's dread words in his will reveal that *he* did not think the subject was amusing. He believed he was being murdered, but he obviously didn't know how it was being done or he would have stopped it.

Arsenic in those days was the poison of choice by murderers, and it *was* present in suspiciously large amounts in Napoleon's hair. But was it an assassination or merely an accident? Perhaps we will never know, but a friend of mine with whom I discussed this mystery reminded me of Oscar Wilde's last words on *his* deathbed in a dingy Paris boardinghouse:

"Either that wallpaper goes or I go."

DID HITLER ESCAPE?

1

A mystery that emerged from the caldron of World War II may at last be solved. So far it has attracted little attention, but if my friend forensic odontologist Lester Luntz, D.D.S., continues his efforts, and he plans to do so, the world is in for a shock.

The mystery is this: Did Adolf Hitler, Germany's fanatical dictator, survive the war and escape?

To ask the question is to invite ridicule. Western historians, basing their conclusions on "eyewitness" accounts, have said for years that Hitler and Eva Braun committed suicide in a bunker beneath wartorn Berlin. Then their bodies were doused with gasoline and burned in the garden of the Reich Chancellery above. But not long after the last smoke cleared over the ruins of Berlin, Soviet leaders, from General Zhukov to dictator Joseph Stalin, hinted that Hitler had escaped.

What actually happened on April 30, 1945? Did Adolf Hitler die?

2

In April 1945, the proud German Army that had once thundered across Europe, then probed deep into Russia, was reduced to a few divisions of men fighting a last-ditch battle in Berlin against the Allies. Adolf Hitler commanded this defense from a fortified bunker deep underground, huddled together with his closest cronies and aides as artillery shells exploded overhead.

Each day smartly uniformed Nazi generals marched into the bunker and gathered around military maps with the Führer. As red lines indicating the Russian envelopment of the city drew closer, the generals could no longer hide the truth of defeat. And on April 21, 1945, in a conference never forgotten by its participants, Adolf Hitler went into a frenzy. He threw down his pencil on the table, white-faced, then screamed at the frightened generals, "Then it's finished? The war is lost!"

From that day, his aides later testified, Hitler began making plans to kill himself. He told them he did not intend to be dragged through Moscow streets in a cage, exhibited like an ape. Instead, he discussed a suicide through poison with his doctors, who recommended potassium cyanide because it acted so swiftly. And in a scene perhaps symbolic of Hitler's ruthlessness (or "iron will," as his fanatical followers believed), he had the poison administered to his faithful dog, Blondi, who twitched violently, and died. It was said that when Hitler was called in to see his dead pet on the floor, he merely nodded and, face expressionless, retired from the room.

In those last desperate days aides pleaded with Hitler to escape. Hans Bauer, undoubtedly one of the most skillful aviators the world has ever known, had been landing and taking off from the street outside the Reich Chancellery, the Wilhelmstrasse. He told Hitler he could fly him to an airbase in northern Germany, and from there he could travel by a long-range German Army transport plane into hiding in a far-off country. Martin Bormann, his deputy, and others pleaded with the Führer to fly to Berchtesgaden, his villa in the Alps, where German troops could guard him in those almost impenetrable mountains.

But Hitler, according to aides who survived, said no; he had determined to die in Berlin. The idea of suicide by the Führer saddened his followers, but did not surprise them. The Hitler they knew in the bunker was entirely different from the dynamic leader who had single-handedly galvanized the German people and led them into war. Now the Führer was weak-looking, graying, ashen-faced, and his left arm trembled so violently that he sometimes had to hold it still with his other hand.

His Nazi cronies believed the transformation was not because of the pressures of war, or even the sting of defeat, but instead was due to the exotic pep-up drugs administered to Hitler daily by Dr. Theodore Morell, perhaps the original "Dr. Feelgood." Morell was scorned by the legitimate doctors who also attended Hitler.

Day by day, night by night, the Russians drew

closer. The Battle of Berlin was a fierce war, fought among rubble which gave excellent protection to the defenders. But the massive might of the Red Army, with Stalin's "organ grinders" firing multiple artillery shells into the heart of the city, took its toll.

With defeat inevitable, Hitler took two final steps. He gave permission to his Nazi followers to break out of the bunker and attempt to escape after he died. And he made the dreams of his longtime mistress, Eva Braun, come true. He married her, less than twenty-four hours before they were to die together.

On the afternoon of April 30, Adolf Hitler and Eva Braun retired to Hitler's living room in the bunker. Hitler had a Walther 7.65-caliber pistol, Eva a smaller one. They each had two cyanide pills. Hitler had been told to place the pistol to his temple, and bite down on the cyanide pill as he pulled the trigger. Eva would simply take the poison.

Our knowledge of what happened next arises from conflicting testimony of witnesses. We are not even certain which aides waited outside the door. Among them, reportedly, were Major Otto Gunsche, Hitler's adjutant, Heinz Linge, his valet, Martin Bormann, his deputy, and Arthur Axmann, Nazi Youth leader. Most historians agree Gunsche and Linge were certainly present. But Erich Klempka, Hitler's chauffeur, for example, was one of the few of the bunker's inhabitants to escape the Russians and land in Allied lands, and his "eyewitness" account was heavily relied upon by Western historians. Yet twenty-five years later he admitted he was not even inside the bunker at the time.

According to other of the "bunker people" interrogated later by Western authorities, after returning from Soviet prisons, this is what happened at the time of Hitler's death. First of all, interestingly, *no one ever heard a shot*. This fact puzzled them, and their only explanation was that Hitler's room had a heavy steel door. They waited nervously for ten minutes, then entered the room, where they found Hitler slumped on one side of the sofa (one witness said he was in an armchair), blood running from his temple (one said left temple, another, right), a gun at his feet. Eva Braun was slumped on the other side of the couch. A smell of bitter almonds characteristic of potassium cyanide was in the room. They wrapped the bodies in blankets and carried them up the staircase which led to a door on ground level opening onto the Reich Chancellery garden. There they placed the two bodies in a shallow trench, doused them with gasoline, and set them afire with a flaming rag.

It was a grisly, perhaps fitting end for the Nazi empire: a few forlorn fanatics huddling in a dark doorway as artillery shells exploded nearby, forcing them to duck inside the building from time to time for protection. They watched a roaring sea of flame consume the Führer who had once ruled with such might and ceremony. But the charred, unrecognizable bodies of Hitler and Eva Braun were never buried. The shell fire made it impossible for his aides to remain exposed aboveground long enough to do the job.

And thus Adolf Hitler died.

Or did he?

4

Allied troops poised outside Berlin wondered what had become of Hitler. A German radio report on April 30 had said that the Führer had died in action, leading his troops in battle. But the Russians, who now controlled the German capital, said the Nazi dictator had not died. He had escaped. According to an electrifying report published in *Time* magazine:

> A team of Soviet detectives concluded last week that if Adolf Hitler was dead, he had not died in the ruins of his Reich Chancellery.
>   . . . Behind the bookcase in Hitler's personal room in the battle-wrecked Chancellery, the sleuths found a thin, concrete, removable panel. Behind it was a man-size hole leading to a super-secret concrete shelter far underground and 500 meters away. Another tunnel connected the shelter with an underground trolley line.
>   . . . In a corridor leading to the secret shelter, the detectives found a charred note in a woman's handwriting. It told her parents not to worry if they did not hear from her for a long while. The Soviet investigators thought that Eva Braun had written it.

On May 26, just weeks after the end of the war, Harry Hopkins, a special adviser to U.S. President Harry Truman, arrived in Moscow to confer with Stalin on problems concerning the founding of the United Nations. Stalin told Hopkins that the Russians had not found Hitler's body. "In my opinion Hitler is not dead, but is hiding somewhere."

Ten days later, on June 6, Soviet Marshal Zhukov held a press conference in Berlin. When Western reporters pressed him to explain what had happened to Hitler, Zhukov commented, "I can say nothing definite about his fate. He could have flown away from Berlin at the very last moment. The state of the runway would have allowed him to do so."

It was said the press sat dazed after this revelation. Adolf Hitler might have escaped? The resulting uproar in the world press caused the British government to launch its own investigation of Hitler's fate. It uncovered the chauffeur, Klempka, who claimed he had been in the bunker when Hitler committed suicide, and Herman Karnov, a German policeman who had seen, from the Reich Chancellery roof, the bodies of Hitler and Eva Braun burning. "I recognized the Führer by his mustache and Eva Braun by her peculiar black shoes," he said. But he admitted he couldn't recognize their features because of the flames.

The British government published the results of its investigation in an official report which concluded that Adolf Hitler had shot himself, and that Eva Braun had taken poison. But the report was based on scanty evidence, mainly the testimony of Klempka and Karnov; and in light of Soviet denials that Hitler's body had been found, it was greeted with skepticism.

In this continuing turmoil, England's most respected historian, Hugh Trevor-Roper, attempted to clear up the mystery once and for all. He went to Berlin and discovered that almost all the bunker inhabitants had been captured by the Soviets and imprisoned in Russia. Still, he was able to find "fringe" witnesses, such as guards and soldiers, as well as to interview high-ranking Nazi officers who had not been in the bunker at the time but knew of the events that had taken place there. And, of course, he used the testimony of Klempka and Karnov.

Trevor-Roper published a book, *The Last Days of Hitler,* in which he concluded that Hitler had in fact committed suicide. Such was Trevor-Roper's reputation that, for most people, the book effectively put to rest the belief that he might have survived. Still, the Soviets continued to deny they knew anything about Hitler's fate.

Then in 1968 there was a sensational development. For reasons never explained, Kremlin leaders admitted they had not only recovered the charred corpses of Hitler and Braun on May 4, 1945, five days after their death, but also had conducted autopsies on the bodies and, through odontology (forensic dentistry) had positively identified them as those of the Führer and his wife.

This revelation, complete with pictures and diagrams of the dead man's teeth, was contained in a book, *The Death of Hitler*, by a Soviet historian, Lev Bezymenski. But was it Hitler's body that had been recovered, or a double's? Bezymenski had no doubt it was the Führer's, but his fascinating story of the discovery of the body raised the possibility that doubles might have been used as part of Hitler's security system, or as decoys to enable him to escape. In fact, the first body found by the Russians near the bunker and initially identified as the Führer's was a double's. Meanwhile, a Russian soldier had found the bodies of another man, a woman and two dogs in a nearby crater that was strewn with burned paper. But in the belief that Hitler's body had already been found, the two new corpses were covered in blankets and buried. Later, when it was discovered the first body was not Hitler's but that of a look-alike, the two corpses were dug up again and sent to a Berlin suburb, where autopsies were performed.

Both of the corpses were burned severely, and parts of the cranium were missing in each case. Splinters of glass and parts of a thin-walled capsule were found in the mouths, which, together with the "smell of bitter almonds," convinced the forensic specialists that both the male and the female had poisoned themselves.

But were they really Hitler and Eva Braun?

Charred bodies, as I have learned in my experience with both fires and airplane crashes, are the most difficult to identify. You have indications of height, race, sex and age, and sometimes bones yield evidence of previous fractures which are helpful in identification. But almost always the teeth are the main clue. And there we rely on the science of forensic odontology, by which means surviving teeth and bridges are compared to previous X rays and medical records of dental work to positively identify an anonymous corpse.

In the upper jaw of the corpse tentatively identified as Adolf Hitler's were nine teeth connected by a gold bridge. The lower jaw had fifteen teeth. Soviet forensic scientists removed both the bridge and the lower jaw and delivered them to Soviet Counterintelligence, which was assigned the task of identifying the body.

Hitler's dentist, Dr. Hugo Blashke, had fled, but an assistant, Kathe Heusemann, was found still in Berlin. She was taken to Blashke's clinic, where she was able to locate a card which proved to be the dental history of Adolf Hitler. But there were no X rays. Again with Heusemann's assistance, they were discovered in Blashke's office in the basement of the Chancellery.

Another of Blashke's dental assistants, Fritz Echtmann, was found and interrogated. Shown Hitler's bridge and lower jaw, which the Russians had placed unceremoniously in a cigar box, both Heusemann and Echtmann identified them "unequivocally" as Hitler's. Furthermore, a gold bridge taken from the mouth of the female corpse was identified "without hesitancy" as belonging to Eva Braun.

The Soviet book should have settled the question of Hitler's death once and for all, but it did nothing of the kind. There were too many inconsistencies in it—

and in the official autopsy reports included in its pages. For example, Bezymenski said that the X rays of Hitler's teeth, the most vital tool of identification, were found by the Soviets—but intriguingly the X rays were not published in the book, only pictures of the teeth found on the unidentified corpse.

There was another forensic flaw in the book. The autopsy reports revealed that the corpse contained only one testicle—and none of Hitler's medical records showed him to be a victim of monorchism, as the condition is called. In fact, his doctors vehemently denied it.

Chief among those claiming the book was a fraud was Dr. Erwin Giesing, the last physician to give Adolf Hitler a complete physical examination, after the bomb plot which almost took his life. Giesing denounced the Soviet odontology of Hitler's teeth, and had evidence to back him: an X ray of Hitler's head, including the teeth, taken by himself during his examination of the Führer. There were marked differences between this X ray and Hitler's teeth as they were pictured and described by the Soviets.

In sum, according to Giesing, the corpse with one testicle instead of two, and the wrong teeth, was not and could not be Adolf Hitler's. The Soviets had autopsied the wrong man. Had they autopsied a double? Had they been the victims of a hoax? Or were they perpetuating a hoax themselves?

5

In this climate of confusion, a distinguished American odontologist entered the picture, and apparently settled the question.

Raeder Sognaaes, a professor of anatomy and oral biology at the University of California at Los Angeles, embarked on a personal academic expedition to solve the case. He delivered the results of his research at an international forensic convention in 1972. Noting that neither Trevor-Roper's nor Bezymenski's book had contained any X-ray documentation, Sognaaes said he had realized that his first task was to find such X rays.

Sognaaes was apparently unaware of the X-ray photograph owned by Giesing and published that same year, 1972. Or perhaps he thought Giesing's X rays were not adequate. In any case, his search for X rays led him first to the transcripts of the interrogation of Dr. Hugo Blashke, Hitler's dentist, by the Americans after the war. In it, Blashke described Hitler's teeth from memory, and mentioned X rays of Hitler's head. But he told his American interrogators that his files, including X rays, had been placed on a transport plane bound for Salzburg, which crashed and burned.

Sognaaes did not give up hope. His search led him to a U.S. archives building in Suitland, Maryland, where he looked up the file of Hitler's "Dr. Feelgood," Dr. Theodore Morell. In the table of contents were listed "Annex II: Five X-Rays of Hitler's Head." But Annex II was missing. "However," Sognaaes reported, "separate from the document itself was found a very worn and torn rough pink wartime paper envelope. This, at long last, did indeed reveal the missing links, five X-ray plates marked September 19, 1944, and October 21, 1944, respectively."

Sognaaes now felt he had the forensic evidence he needed. He could compare these antemortem X rays with the Soviet postmortem pictures and autopsy description of Hitler's teeth, and arrive at either an identification of Hitler or proof that the Soviets were wrong.

Sognaaes concluded, from his study of Blashke's interrogation, the X rays he found in Maryland and the Russian postmortem information, that "the accumulated evidence now provides definite odontological proof that Hitler did in fact die, and that the Russians did indeed recover and autopsy the right body."

This impressive, and important, research of a professional forensic odontologist was greeted by the world press as the final answer to the mystery. Only Dr. Giesing in Germany still objected, and with some good reason, it would seem. He had an X ray of his own of Hitler's head which did not correspond to the Soviet pictures and descriptions. But Giesing was an eye, ear, nose and throat specialist, not an odontologist skilled in forensic dentistry, and thus his opinions were discounted.

But the puzzle of Hitler's fate was far from solved.

6

One phase of the continuing mystery began with Sognaaes himself. Almost incredibly, it seems to me, he claimed in 1981 that although the male body found in the trench was Adolf Hitler's, the female body found with him was *not* Eva Braun's. How could that be?

Sognaaes pointed out that one of the pieces of evidence by which Eva was positively identified by the Soviets was a certain dental bridge with white plastic teeth. According to their autopsy report: "On the metal plate of the bridge the first and second artificial white molars are attached in front; their appearance is almost indistinguishable from natural teeth."

If this bridge had actually been in Eva's mouth, Sognaaes said, the plastic teeth would have melted, along with the metal plate. However, the bridge was

not in her mouth. It had never been fitted and was
still in the files of Blashke's office when Eva supposedly died. Thus, Sognaaes believed it likely that the
body found in the Chancellery garden was a substitute, not Eva Braun's, and that the Soviets placed the
bridge on the body after it had been found.

With that revelation, the mystery deepened. For if
the body found in the trench was not Eva Braun, why
should the man found lying beside her be Adolf Hitler? If we are to believe the Nazi witnesses who huddled in a doorway and watched the flames, the two of
them, Hitler and Braun, died together.

Wondering if the mystery would ever be solved, I
was intrigued when I heard that Dr. Lester Luntz,
professor of oral diagnosis at the University of Con-
necticut Dental School, was going to deliver a paper
on the identification of Hitler's body at the 1984 trien-
nial meeting of the International Association of Forensic Sciences in Oxford, England. Luntz had spent
eighteen years on his research, and advance word said
that he was going to refute both the Soviet report and
the Sognaaes report.

In his speech at the conference, Luntz said that the
Soviets, contrary to Bezymenski's book, had not found
Hitler's dental X rays in Blashke's office in the Chancellery. Those X rays had indeed disappeared on a
plane which never reached its destination. And, on
the other hand, the X rays found by Sognaaes in the
U.S. archives, and said by him to be definite proof of
Hitler's identification, were not that at all. For one
thing, Luntz said, the dates handwritten in ink show
a strange and troubling discrepancy. On the alleged
German X rays, "Oct." appears, short for "October."
But if the X rays really were German, the abbreviation
would have been "Okt.," short for the German "Okto-
ber."

"Such questionable evidence is unacceptable for making a positive dental identification," Luntz concluded, adding that in the archives there appeared to have been several sets of original and duplicate X rays. So no one, including Sognaaes, could be certain that the strange envelope he found contained Hitler's X rays or someone else's.

In fact, Luntz believed that the Soviets had autopsied the wrong body, and cited other evidence such as the testimony of Otto Gunsche, Hitler's adjutant, who had told him that the Russians had not found Hitler's body. Gunsche, who was present during those last days in the bunker, should know, Luntz said.

Later that afternoon, in the charming lounge of a small hotel in Oxford, I spoke to Lester Luntz. Usually a lively, loquacious man, Luntz was subdued. For the very day he delivered his paper refuting Sognaaes, the California odontologist died of cancer. This was sad news for Luntz (and for me, as well); like all professionals, he never let an academic dispute darken a friendship.

Luntz told me he was writing a book on his eighteen-year search for the answers to the mystery of Hitler's death, and that the paper he had just delivered merely touched on a few points. He had interviewed many German witnesses and had seen all the documentation, but the only hint he would give me about his new material was: "Sognaaes didn't know that Blashke was a fanatical Nazi."

What the fanatical Nazism of Hitler's dentist meant in terms of the mystery Luntz wouldn't tell me, but he emphasized again that the Soviets had not autopsied Hitler's body.

In sum, Luntz believes, as do many others, that the Soviets did not find the body of the real Hitler. And

Sognaaes before his death claimed that the body identified as Eva Braun's was most likely a substitute.

If one substitute, why not two?

Which brings us back to the days of May 1945 in
wartorn Berlin when Soviet investigators told a news-
magazine reporter of a hidden door which led to an
underground tunnel, and a note found in it which was
apparently left by Eva Braun.

Could it be?

WHO WAS JACK THE RIPPER?

On November 10, 1888, American newspapers published a cable dispatch from London, England, which
evoked the terror of the English people in that Victo-
rian era, and created the legend of a criminal whose
exploits are still spoken of with dread.

> The Whitechapel fiend has committed another butchery
> more horrible than any that has preceded it . . . at ten
> o'clock this morning . . . three horrified policemen who
> had first looked in through Mary Jane Kelly's window,
> and then drank big glasses of brandy to steady them-
> selves, were breaking in her door with a pick-axe. The
> Whitechapel murderer had done his work with more
> thoroughness than ever before. The miserable woman's
> body was literally scattered all over the room. . . . The

butchery was so frightful that more than an hour was spent by the doctors in endeavoring to reconstruct the woman's body from the pieces so as to place it in a coffin and have it photographed.

Mary Jane Kelly was the fifth and last victim of the Whitechapel fiend, known to history as Jack the Ripper. His victims were all prostitutes, most of whom were found with their throats slashed and their internal organs cut out and either strewn around or taken away by the murderer. Mary Jane Kelly's heart, for example, was neatly placed next to her face, her amputated breasts were on a table, and her intestines were draped across a mirror.

The murders brought into the action a most unusual forensic-scientist/detective: Queen Victoria. In a letter to the Home Secretary, she wrote, "The murderer's clothes must be saturated with blood and must be kept somewhere. Have the cattleboats and passenger boats been examined? Has any investigation been made as to the number of single men occupying rooms to themselves? . . . is there sufficient surveillance at night?"

Royal outrage matched the horror in the street, a terror accentuated by taunting letters from the Ripper in which he informed the police that he meant to keep on killing, and nothing could stop him. In a letter to the magistrate at Thames Police Court, he wrote:

DEAR BOSS,
It is no use for you to look for me in London because I'm not there. Don't trouble yourself about me until I return, which will not be very long. I like the work too well to leave it alone. Oh, it was a jolly job, the last one. I had plenty of time to do it properly in. Ha, ha, ha! The

next lot I mean to do with a vengeance, cut off their head
and arms. . . . So goodbye, dear Boss, till I return.
                                                    Yours,
                                         Jack the Ripper

The killings began on August 31, 1888. Mary Ann
Nicholls, a forty-two-year-old prostitute, had been
seen lurking around the streets of the East End,
drunk, trying to raise fourpence for a bed in a lodging-
house. She was later found in an alley, her throat slit
and her internal organs disemboweled. In reporting
the murder, *The Star*, a London newspaper, did not
spare its readers the gory details:

> The knife, which must have been a large and sharp one,
> was jabbed into . . . the lower part of the abdomen and
> then drawn upwards, not once but twice. The first cut
> veered to the right, slitting up the groin, and passing over
> the left hip, but the second cut went straight upward,
> along the centre of the body, and reaching to the breast-
> bone. Such horrible work could only be the deed of a
> maniac!

Nicholls' case was mishandled from the start. A doctor called to the scene merely affirmed that she was
dead and later admitted he had not seen, or realized,
the extent and nature of her injuries. He ordered her
moved to a workhouse mortuary, where the attendant,
a "pauper" with no medical knowledge, cleaned and
washed the body before physicians could examine it
for forensic clues. Meanwhile the bloodstains in the
street were washed off by police before the Chief Inspector of Scotland Yard arrived.

Nevertheless, some clues were found. The policemen testified that there was only a small amount of

blood in the street, a puzzling phenomenon considering the many terrible knife cuts. Could the victim
have been killed elsewhere and dumped there? police wondered. No, because there had been no trail of
blood which would indicate that the body had been
dragged to the spot, and no marks of wheels in the
road. Also a doctor who examined the body stated,
"There was very little blood around the neck, and
there were no marks of any struggle."

The doctor also made these forensic points: The
knife slashes were made "from left to right and might
have been done by a left-handed person." The
weapon, he said, was a very long-bladed knife, adding
that it was possibly a "cork-cutter's or shoemaker's
knife." And he remarked that the mutilations were
"deftly and fairly skillfully performed."

The second murder provided more clues. Eight
days after Nicholls' killing, on September 8, 1888,
Anne Chapman, another prostitute, with the picturesque nickname "Dark Annie," was found on a street
in the same neighborhood, even more horribly butchered than the previous victim.

Once again there was the curious phenomenon of
only a little blood found at the scene, and no evidence
that the body had been dumped there. But this time
the killer had deliberately left clues. A few pennies,
two farthings, and two brass rings taken from the victim's fingers were placed neatly at her feet. A portion
of a bloodstained envelope bearing the name of the
Sussex Regiment and postmarked "London, 28 August, 1888" was also found, but the address was missing.

Surprisingly, the victim's clothes were not torn, but
another garment caught the police inspector's attention: a leather apron hanging nearby. It was saturated

with water, but revealed no bloodstains. Butchers and slaughterhouse workers wore leather aprons, and indeed a slaughterhouse was in the vicinity.

Once again the physician who conducted the post-mortem examination complained about what had been done to the body before his arrival. Dr. Bagster Phillips revealed that the body had not even been taken to a mortuary; instead it was carried to a shed and cleaned and washed before he could examine it.

Nevertheless he detected some differences between the two killings. Nicholls' throat had been slashed; Chapman's had been cut clear through, the head almost severed. And, most grimly, the second victim's kidney and ovaries had been removed. The killer had taken them with him.

Dr. Phillips said that the cutting out of the internal organs revealed "indications of anatomical knowledge." He added that the wounds indicated "a very sharp knife with a thin, narrow blade . . . six to eight inches in length" or even longer. He speculated that the weapon was either a physician's surgical instrument or a bayonet.

As yet there had been no eyewitness sightings of any men with the two victims, but, based on the forensic evidence of the knife and the leather apron, police concentrated their search on the slaughterhouse and butcher shops in the area. Suspects were turned up, but all had alibis. Meanwhile, at an inquest Dr. Phillips emphasized the "deliberate . . . and apparently scientific manner in which the poor woman was mutilated . . . I myself could not have performed such surgery, even working at top speed, under a quarter of an hour. . . . No unskilled person could have done this. It must have been someone used to the post-mortem room."

On September 30, just three weeks later, the famous "double event" occurred: two murders within an hour. The killer was obviously interrupted before he could mutilate Elizabeth Stride, although he did slash her throat. An hour later he found and killed another victim, Katherine Eddowes, and this time proceeded with his characteristic disembowelling and mutilation.

Not far away from the scene of the second crime, police found bloodstained water in a sink in a narrow passage off the street. The killer had obviously stopped to wash his hands. But, even more importantly, the Ripper had taken a piece of Eddowes' apron to wipe his hands, and this bloodstained fabric was found in the doorway of a nearby house. And there the Ripper left a message which haunts the killings to this day. On the wall inside the doorway the following words were found written in chalk: "THE JUWES ARE NOT THE MEN TO BE BLAMED FOR NOTHING."

"Juwes?" Was that a misspelling for "Jews?" If so, did it mean the Ripper was Jewish, or that he wanted to mislead the police into believing so? Whatever his motive, the writing of the message itself, including the possible identification of the chalk and analysis of the printing style, was destroyed by none other than Sir Charles Warren, the bumbling Police Commissioner. He ordered the message to be wiped off the wall immediately.

In the words of a junior officer at Scotland Yard, "The metropolitan police held the clue to the identification of the murderer in their own hands and deliberately threw it away under the personal direction of the Commissioner of Police, who acted in the belief that an anti-Semitic riot might take place."

There was, however, a break in the case. This time

witnesses had seen a man with each of the victims, and the descriptions were almost identical. Seen with Stride was "a man, age 28, height five feet eight inches, dark complexion, small dark moustache, black diagonal coat, hard felt hat, collar and tie; respectable appearance." Seen with Eddowes was a man age thirty, height five feet seven or eight inches, mustache fair, medium build, but he was not as formally dressed. Instead of a collar and tie he wore a reddish neckerchief under a loose jacket.

Other witnesses claimed they saw a well-dressed man carrying a "shiny black bag," and decades later, in 1931, Robert Clifford Spicer claimed that, as a constable that night, he had arrested just such a man around 2 A.M. The man was sitting on a dustbin in an alley with a prostitute named Rosy who had two shillings in her hand. But at the local police station the inspector informed Spicer that his suspect was a highly respected doctor with an address in Brixton, and the man was released even though Spicer asked what a respectable physician was doing sitting on a dustbin with a prostitute in a dark alley.

Meanwhile, the taunting letters from Jack the Ripper had begun. To this day there is controversy over the authenticity of the letters, but one of them was accompanied by a gruesome bit of evidence in a cardboard box: a portion of a kidney. The letter said: "From Hell . . . I send you half the kidne [sic] I took from one woman, preserved to you, tother piece I fried and ate it, it was very nice."

The curator of the London Hospital Museum examined the organ and stated that it was a portion of the kidney of someone who drank alcohol heavily. "I should say it belonged to a woman aged about forty-five and had been removed from the body within the last two weeks." The left kidney of Katherine Eddowes, a heavy drinker about forty-two years of age, had been taken away by the Ripper after her murder less than two weeks before.

The fifth and last murder by the Ripper showed some differences from the others. Mary Jane Kelly, the victim, was young and pretty, only twenty-five, whereas the other prostitutes were aged forty to forty-five. Secondly, she was the only one of the victims to be killed indoors, in her room, instead of in a dark alley. But, like the others, she was a prostitute and a known heavy drinker.

At 2 A.M. on November 30, 1888, George Hutchinson, a laborer, had no place to sleep. He saw a man standing at the corner of Whitechapel Road and Commercial Street, but paid little attention to him because pretty Mary Kelly was approaching. He had always fancied Mary, but never had the money to afford her. Now she asked to "borrow" sixpence, her way of soliciting, but Hutchinson had to admit he didn't possess even this small sum.

Mary Kelly said that in that case she would have to look for money elsewhere, and walked across the street to the man on the corner. Jealous, Hutchinson looked more closely at the man and, as he told police later, his suspicions were immediately aroused because it was unusual to see so "well-dressed" a man in the East End.

If Hutchinson's eyewitness account is accepted as truth, then his was the first real look at Jack the Ripper, because Kelly's murder took place shortly after the man and the girl walked toward her house, watched by the jealous Hutchinson. In the earlier eyewitness accounts, the sightings of possible suspects were not closely linked in time or place to the killings.

The man, according to Hutchinson, was about five

feet six inches in height, dark complected, with heavy eyebrows and a thick mustache which curled at the ends. He wore a soft felt hat, a long dark coat, a black tie fastened with a horseshoe tiepin, and spats over buttoned shoes. Hutchinson thought he looked like a foreigner. Ominously, the man carried in his left hand a thin parcel about eight inches long.

Pretty and saucy Mary Kelly was butchered more cruelly than any of the others. And this time another puzzling clue emerged. Kelly's room contained a fireplace, and the grate was still warm when police arrived in the morning. Obviously a fire had burned in it late at night. In its ashes were a *woman's* felt hat, a *woman's* clothing, and a piece of burnt velvet.

Mary Kelly's clothes were neatly stacked in a pile by the bed, so whose clothes had been burned? And why burn them unless they were bloodstained? Was it possible that Jack the Ripper was a woman and thus had been able to elude detection? And what class of woman would have anatomical knowledge? Midwives, police knew.

But another answer to the clue of the fire occurred to police. Doctors who examined Mary Kelly's remains concluded that it would have taken the Ripper two to two and a half hours to accomplish his mutilation. In that time he needed light and a fire. Mary Kelly was too poor to own firewood, so the Ripper had used her other clothes to make a fire that would provide light and keep him warm while he concluded his grisly work.

Modern forensic science was in its infancy in the 1880s. Still, by examination of the wounds of all of the Ripper's victims, police surgeons were able not only to describe the type of weapon, a long thin knife, but to narrow the field of suspects to someone who had a knowledge of surgical cutting as well as of the locations of anatomical organs. This, together with eyewitness descriptions of a "well-dressed" man, led police to discard the notion of a slaughterhouse worker or a butcher, and to begin searching among the better classes for a physician, or a layman with medical knowledge.

By coincidence, a play based on the novel *Dr. Jekyll and Mr. Hyde* by Robert Louis Stevenson had opened in London at this time and suggested the possibility that a "normal" man might also be a sadistic killer. But police apparently were loath to concede that the killer was a "normal" *Englishman.* Instead they focused their suspicions on a Pole named Severin Klosowski and a Russian named Alexander Pedachenko.

Severin Klosowski, the Pole, had been in his native country a *feldscher,* an assistant to a doctor. In London he was a barber's assistant. Police pointed out that in Europe the local barber was the poor man's doctor, often performing minor surgery. Thus Klosowski would have knowledge of surgical technique. Moreover, he physically resembled the description of eyewitnesses, even to the mustache curled at the ends. And he was known as a "ladies' man," drifting from woman to woman.

Klosowski was not arrested for the Ripper's crimes. In 1890 he left for the United States with a wife and settled in Jersey City, where, very soon after, a Jack the Ripper–type murder occurred. Two years later he returned to England, using the name George Chapman. The police had lost track of him until it was learned that three of this wives, one after the other, had died suddenly, suffering from violent stomach cramps.

Whether or not he was Jack the Ripper, Chapman became a legend in forensic-science history, because it was at his trial that the first chemical analysis of poison by forensic scientists in England resulted in the conviction of a killer. The poison was antimony.

Scotland Yard was certain that Jack the Ripper and George Chapman were the same man, but many students of the case disagree. For one thing, Klosowski was only twenty-three at the time of the murders, not thirty or thirty-five. Also, his mode of crime was to marry a woman, take her money, then dispose of her quietly by poison, not mutilation.

To further confuse the issue, it was discovered that Klosowski had a "double" in London, a Russian who was also a barber-surgeon. The police never named the man, but an author, William Le Queux, a former British Secret Service agent, revealed the name Alexander Pedachenko. His source was, of all people, Rasputin, the fanatical monk who was so powerful in the court of the Tsar of Russia. Le Queux claimed that the Kerensky government in Russia gave him documents found in Rasputin's house so that he could write an exposé of the friend of the deposed Tsar. Among them was a manuscript labeled "Great Russian Criminals" which said that Pedachenko, "the greatest and boldest of all Russian criminal lunatics, was encouraged to go to London and commit that series of atrocious crimes." The motive, according to Rasputin, was to bring discredit on the Russian emigré revolutionaries who lived in the East End. And that, it was thought, might explain the chalked message about "the Juwes."

Police searching for Pedachenko went to a certain basement and there found Klosowski (before he left for America). The two men were remarkably similar in appearance and often used to assume each other's identity. The coincidence of the two look-alikes was never explained, and Pedachenko eventually went back to Russia, according to Rasputin.

Or did he drown? For years police officials told many people, off the record, that Jack the Ripper was a Russian surgeon who had been found drowned in the Thames a month after the last killing. Nevertheless the official search continued, and the names of new suspects emerged, ranging from an American doctor to the Duke of Clarence, King Edward VII's eldest son, who was allegedly insane.

A few years ago I journeyed to Wichita, Kansas, with other pathologists to speak at a seminar on Jack the Ripper organized by Bill Eckert, a forensic historian and head of INFORM, the clearinghouse for information on forensic subjects. We discussed what modern forensic science could have done to assist the police in their search for the identity of Jack the Ripper.

Fingerprinting, blood-typing, hair and fiber analysis, and many other modern procedures were not available to the surgeons who examined the victims in 1888. If they had been, there is no doubt in my mind that Jack the Ripper would have been caught. For example, the piece of Katherine Eddowes' apron found in the doorway must have contained fingerprints. The Ripper had apparently used the cloth to wipe his bloodstained hands after the murder.

Secondly, some of the victims might have fought back before death, and caused scratches on their assailant's face or neck. Often, tiny rolls of skin are found under a victim's fingernails and can aid in the identification of a murderer. Further, if the assailant had somehow been cut, an analysis of the bloodstains in the area might have revealed his blood, and typing the blood could have narrowed the field of suspects. Also, the analysis of semen stains, if any, would have assisted in locating the killer.

As to speculations that the killer was a woman ("Jill the Ripper," as one newspaper said), there are even blood analysis procedures which can distinguish female blood from male, although they are so new that the courts have not yet accepted them.

The surgeons in 1888 were able to describe Jack the Ripper's knife, but nowadays we can actually *reproduce* the weapon's blade by pouring a hot waxlike substance into the wound and waiting until it cools. London police could have taken such a replica to various shops which sold knives, and also could have compared it physically to surgical or slaughterhouse knives.

If the killer bit his victim, modern dental odontology could have recreated his teeth. And finally, of course, hair from the killer's head, as well as fibers from his clothing, would almost certainly be found at the scene of such violent crimes, and they could have led to positive identification.

In Wichita we also discussed the strange phenomenon of so little blood at the scene of the butchery. The surgeons in 1888 believed that the killer clapped his hand over his victim's mouth, then slit her throat. But the lack of blood indicates she was dead before the knifing began, so we believed she was strangled first, and then the mutilation began.

In 1992 the English government will at last open Scotland Yard's files on Jack the Ripper, and we can expect a fresh surge of speculation on the case of the most famous criminal of all time. If those files contain original documents and evidence, forensic science may yet play a role in identifying the immortal Jack the Ripper.

THE RETURN OF THE RIPPER

Almost a century after Jack the Ripper terrorized London, a series of nearly identical murders occurred in England. Once again the victims were prostitutes in inner-city slums who were savagely mutilated and, just as in the 1890s, police received taunting letters from someone who signed his name "The Ripper."

Because of television and other means of instant communication which swiftly, and graphically, circulated the news of the murders, the new Ripper's deeds inspired even more widespread horror than Jack's. And the public was right to be afraid, for this "Ripper" did not stop after five murders; he eventually killed thirteen young women in his murderous rampage.

The killing spree began on October 29, 1975, in Leeds, an industrial city in northern England. Chapeltown, an inner-city ghetto of Leeds with seedy bars and pubs, was the area in which Wilma McCann earned her living as a prostitute. Dressed in a pink blouse, blue bolero jacket and white slacks, McCann made the rounds of pubs that night and was intoxi-

cated when she emerged from the last one, the Room
At The Top, shortly before one o'clock.

The next morning a milkman spotted a body in the
Prince Philip playing fields. Wilma McCann's white
slacks were down around her knees, and her brassiere
had been moved up to expose her breasts. She had
been stabbed in the lower abdomen and chest thirteen times, and her head had been crushed with hammer blows. Despite the sexual overtones of the crime
scene, there was no evidence of sexual activity.

Less than three months later, on January 21, 1976,
another prostitute, Emily Jackson, was found murdered in Leeds in an even more brutal manner. This
time in addition to the crushed skull there were no
fewer than fifty-two stab wounds, and the killer had
thrust a piece of wood between her legs.

The murders of these two prostitutes received little
press coverage, and no connection was made between
the deaths. Indeed, they were almost forgotten, until
on February 5, 1977, the killer struck again in Chapeltown, smashing Irene Richardson's head with a hammer, and stabbing her so viciously that her intestines
spilled out. Once again the clothing of the victim had
been pushed around to reveal her sexual parts, although no evidence of sexual activity was found.

My friend and colleague Professor David Gee of
Leeds University's Department of Forensic Science
was the man who first realized the connection between the killings. He performed the autopsies on all
three victims and saw the forensic "signature" of a
single killer: the identical modes of death, hammer
blows plus stabbing of the chest and the lower abdomen, as well as the clothing moved to reveal sexual
parts even though no rape had taken place. When Dr.
Gee revealed his findings, the press dubbed the killer

"the Yorkshire Ripper," and a new legend in the annals of serial crime was created.

In April of that same year, there was another slaughter in Chapeltown, this time of a streetwalker named Jayne MacDonald, whose body, in addition to the usual wounds, had a broken bottle embedded in her chest. The public now demanded action, and police launched a massive manhunt. Hundreds of people were interrogated, prostitutes were cautioned, a mobile police post was established in Chapeltown, and plainclothesmen fanned out through the area at night.

Then the Ripper struck again. Maureen Long was intoxicated as she walked along Manningham Lane in Leeds at about 2 A.M. on July 9, 1977. A man in a car offered her a lift and she accepted. When she proposed sex for money, he agreed and took her to a waste ground on Randle Street near her home. Once she was out of the car, he struck her with a hammer and stabbed her in the stomach, the chest and the back. He rearranged her clothes, as usual, then left her for dead.

But Maureen Long didn't die, and police finally had a witness who could describe the anonymous killer. Long told them that he was about thirty-seven years old, over six feet tall, and had long blond hair. Ironically, her description turned out to be far off the mark and impeded the investigation, as detectives overlooked potential suspects who did not fit it.

The Ripper had been fortunate, but then he made a second mistake. On October 9, 1977, in his next encounter with a prostitute, Jean Jordan, in Manchester, a city near Leeds, he gave her a five-pound note in advance, and forgot it after he murdered her. Later he realized that this note was newly minted and taken from his pay packet at his place of employment, so it might be traced. But once again fate seemed to smile on the Yorkshire Ripper. The body hidden in bushes had not been found after a week. Emboldened, he decided to return to the scene of the crime and retrieve the note. But when he did so, he found the body but not her purse, and left empty-handed.

Five days later when the police discovered the body, they also found her handbag containing the five-pound note. Immediately they realized the significance of the banknote and started on its trail. The note could not be traced to one man, but it could narrow the field to employees of companies which had received a certain batch of currency from a subbranch of the Medford Bank in Shipley. Eventually the police interviewed eight thousand men, including the Ripper, but his wife assured the police that on the night of the murder he had been home in bed with her.

And so the killings went on. Helen Rytka, eighteen, was the next victim, and the Ripper, in a break with his custom, raped her before stabbing her to death. In doing so, he left evidence of semen. In the 1890s forensic science could have done nothing with such evidence. But in 1977 forensic scientists on the case, led by Dr. Gee, quickly analyzed the semen stains and discovered the Ripper's blood type. It turned out to be Type B, which is found in only six percent of the population in Britain.

Furthermore, footprints in bloody areas near the bodies of his victims had been measured, so Dr. Gee knew the Ripper's foot size. The wounds had been analyzed, enabling Dr. Gee to describe the weapons —a ball-peen hammer, knives and a Phillips screwdriver. And tire tracks had been found which could eventually identify his car. Gradually, forensic science was homing in on the killer—and then the murder of his next victim, Josephine Whittaker, left yet another critical forensic clue. Tiny metallic particles and machine oil were found in the wounds of Whittaker's body. From this clue Dr. Gee knew that the Ripper worked around machinery.

But just at that time the case was sidetracked by a series of letters signed "Jack the Ripper," and a tape recording. The letters were similar to those received by a puzzled police force ninety years before, as was the tape, which began, tauntingly, "I'm Jack. I see you are having no luck catching me." Police not only took the letters and the tape seriously, they also played the tape on national television and radio. The voice on the tape had a peculiar accent associated with a small mining town called Wearside, and police told detectives to disregard all suspects without such an accent. Unfortunately, the tape was fraudulent.

And so the killings went on and on, even as the police manhunt escalated into the largest criminal investigation in England's history. By August 1979 police said that almost 200,000 people had been searched, and more than 22,000 statements were in the files.

Meanwhile, forensic scientists had attacked the authenticity of both the letters and the tape, in which police put so much store. They discovered that everything mentioned in the letters had been printed in the press and so was available to the public. Furthermore, the very similarity of the letters to those of the original Jack the Ripper indicated a hoax.

Nevertheless, police higher-ups doggedly stuck to their belief in the authenticity of the letters and the tape, and their stubbornness once again impeded the investigation. In January 1980, the police, still track-

ing the five-pound note, had narrowed the companies
involved to three, one of which, T. & W. H. Clark Ltd.
of Carol Road, Shipley, employed the Ripper, who
was interrogated for a second time. On that very day,
he was wearing boots which could have incriminated
him because Dr. Gee had discovered the footprint of
a boot at the scene of the Josephine Whittaker killing,
and they could have been compared. But once again
his lack of the odd accent of the voice on the tape led
police to dismiss him as a real suspect.

In November 1980 a college student, Jacqueline
Hill, was murdered, and on January 2, 1981, the Ripper went out on another killing mission. This time,
worried about police surveillance of the red-light
areas in Leeds and nearby towns, he drove to an automobile scrapyard, stole some license plates, and
taped them over the plates of his own Rover. Then he
drove to Sheffield, about thirty miles from Leeds, and
cruised the seedy area of the city. There he picked up
a young black woman (whose name was not revealed
by police) and drove her to a private road of a large
estate. But while he attempted to have sex with her in
the front seat, a police car cruising the area drove up.

The police checked the license plates by radio and
immediately discovered they belonged to a Skoda,
not a Rover. The Ripper was in trouble, yet once again
he pressed his luck. Persuading the police that he
wanted to "take a pee," he secreted his weapons—the
ball-peen hammer and the single-bladed knife—on
his person and hid them behind a small fuel storage
tank on the estate. This left only a small wood-han-
dled knife to dispose of, which he did at the police
station in a cistern.

Under interrogation, the cunning Ripper offered a
plausible explanation for the stolen plates. He was

due in court on a drunk-driving charge in a week and his insurance had just lapsed, so he had hoped to disguise his car with false plates. But good detective work finally came to the fore, aided by forensic science. Police discovered that the young man had been interrogated no fewer than five times in connection with the investigation of the five-pound note and were suspicious. They went back to the place where they had arrested the Ripper and found the hammer and the knife, which fit the descriptions of the weapons that Dr. Gee had provided. Furthermore, his foot size measured at the police station was the same as the boot mark found at the scene of Josephine Whittaker's death.

Meanwhile, in addition to the weapons recovered in the bushes, screwdrivers which also matched the wounds analyzed by Dr. Gee were found in the Ripper's house. As a detective later put it, "We knew the killer's boot size because the Ripper had left footprints in pools of blood; we knew the various types of cars the killer had driven because of tire tracks found at the murder sites; we knew the Ripper's blood type based on semen tests; we knew his weapons, and his connection to the five-pound note."

Confronted with the incriminating evidence, the Ripper finally lost his composure and confessed. "I am the Yorkshire Ripper," he said, and a whole nation breathed a sigh of releif.

Who was the monster, the "Yorkshire Ripper?" He was Peter William Sutcliffe, a man of thirty-five, described by police as "average-looking," who came from a highly respectable family whose financial fortunes had run downhill. Sutcliffe worked as a truck driver with the T. & W. H. Clark Company (accounting for the machine oil found in the wounds on the body of one of the victims). He also sang regularly in the choir at church and was, by all accounts, a happily married man.

Probably no one will ever know the motives for the original Jack the Ripper's killing rampage, but we do know the Yorkshire Ripper's motive. It seems the slaughter of thirteen women was precipitated by anger over a prostitute by whom he was "ripped off" for the grand sum of ten pounds. Or so he told police in his initial interrogation. He later pleaded insanity at his trial, but was convicted of the murder of thirteen people and sentenced to life imprisonment.

It was a victory for police who, duped at first by an inaccurate description and a fraudulent tape and letters, finally captured the Ripper through thorough surveillance procedures. It was an even greater victory for forensic science. While the identity of Jack the Ripper may forever remain a mystery, the forensic evidence collected against the Yorkshire Ripper left him no alternative but to confess.

THE DANGLING MAN
The Case of Roberto Calvi, "the Vatican Banker"

1

Anthony Huntley trod briskly across Blackfriars Bridge in London at 7 A.M. on June 18, 1982, on his way to work as a postal clerk at the *Daily Express*, enjoying the early-morning breeze that slipped north along the Thames. Idly, he glanced down at the river, and stopped. It seemed impossible to believe, but he was looking at the top of the head of a man. What's more, the man was suspended by the neck with an orange nylon rope tied to a makeshift iron scaffolding near the stone embankment of the river.

Perhaps it is a comment on our video age that Huntley did not immediately shout for police. Instead, as he later testified, he was aware that motion pictures were constantly being filmed around London and thought the hanging figure might be a prop for a Hitchcock-style thriller. But when he arrived at his office and told a fellow worker of the grim sight, a telephone call quickly went to Scotland Yard.

Soon a boat bearing London's River Police nudged

the bottom rungs of the iron scaffolding, rocking in the slight swells. Dangling there was a sixtyish man dressed in an expensive suit, with his shoes and ankles under water and a rope around his neck. The police swiftly cut him down, placed him on the deck of the boat and examined him for identification. The first things they discovered were stones stuffed into the pockets of his suit, and a brick tucked into the front of his trousers. Elsewhere in his pockets were $15,000 in various currencies, and a soggy Italian passport.

The name listed in the passport was Gian Roberto Calvini, who had entered the country a few days earlier. A check with Italian authorities revealed that no such passport had ever been issued. But the forged name itself was a clue, because it was so close to the real name of a man the Italian police were looking for.

A day after the death, shock waves rolled through the financial centers of every continent as a Scotland Yard official stood in front of a mass of reporters and announced the real identity of the dangling man: Roberto Calvi. The millionaire known as the "Vatican banker," who guided the Catholic Church in its vast investments and was the respected financial counselor to His Holiness, the Pope, had ended his life dangling above the Thames.

Why? And had he hanged himself, or was it murder?

2

Roberto Calvi was born in the northern-Italian industrial city of Milan in 1920, the same year his future mentor, Michele Sindona, was being ushered into life in Patti, Sicily. Calvi's father, Giacomo, was a man of some distinction. One of the first graduates of Milan's Bocconi University, which specialized in economics, he was recruited by the largest banking institution in Milan, the Banca Commerciale Italiana. Eventually he became joint manager of the bank, a middle-level executive position.

As a child Roberto lived in the wealthiest area of the city and attended private schools, where he proved adept at languages, not only classical Latin and Greek but also French and German. He was remembered by classmates as a shy, reserved boy, but, like many such youngsters, he proved rebellious. His father invited Roberto to go to Bocconi University to follow in his footsteps as a banker. Instead, Roberto in 1939 joined the Army. An angry father saw his son enroll in Pinerola, a training school for cavalry officers.

It is fair to acknowledge that this future banker, who would someday become best remembered as a plump corpse under a London bridge, was a war hero when young. From 1941 to 1943 he fought with honor in the Russian campaign, the most bitter of World War II, enduring subzero winters and massive battles in a hostile land. Then he returned to fight for his own country in the mountains of Italy against the Allied troops.

When the war was over, Calvi's father procured him a clerk's job in a branch of the Banca Commerciale in southern Italy. Then an opening occurred in the Banca Ambrosiana in Milan, and, through his father's influence, Calvi was hired as a junior officer. Banca Ambrosiana was known as a "Catholic" bank, founded before the turn of the century with the help of the Vatican, and still closely connected to the Church. In fact, Ambrosiana was referred to as "the priests' bank."

Calvi had shown bravery in the war; now he revealed talent as a banker. He soon caught the eye of his superiors, and was promoted time and again to ever higher positions. The turning point in his career came in 1960 when he created the country's first mutual fund, Interitalia, and then engineered the purchase of Banca del Battordo, which was to become one of the largest banks in Switzerland. By 1965, Calvi was given the title of central manager of the bank, one of its top positions.

But traditionally the office of bank chairman was reserved for a man with important connections. Calvi, son of a midlevel banker, had none in the upper echelons of the establishment. His road to the top of his profession was apparently blocked forever—until he was discovered by another banker on the rise, Michele Sindona, from Sicily.

Unlike Calvi, Michele Sindona had contacts, of all sorts, and thus had risen both farther and faster in the banking world. His power base, it was said, was founded on two mighty institutions, the Mafia and the Catholic Church.

Sindona began his career as a lawyer in Sicily, then moved to Milan, arriving with a letter of introduction from a bishop in Sicily to a Vatican official, Giovanni Battista Montini, who took a liking to the young Sicilian. When Montini (the future Pope Paul VI) was appointed Archbishop of Milan, Sindona's status in Milan rose sharply. Soon he was buying and selling properties and became rich. Among his investments was the Banca Priola, a small bank in Milan which almost immediately became large because it began receiving deposits from the Vatican's own bank, the

Istituto per le Opere de Religione (IOR). Banca Priola was shortly followed by the acquisition of a second bank, Banca Unione—both of them, of course, closely connected to the Vatican.

By this time Sindona had been appointed a Vatican financial adviser. But he was a man always under a cloud. Newspapers reported that he had never given up his ties to the Mafia from his native Sicily, and by now he was also involved with another shadowy underworld. He belonged to a secret lodge called Propaganda Due, P-2, headed by a sinister figure, Licio Gelli.

P-2 had been founded in the 1800s with the birth of the secret society known as the Carbonari. While its rituals were similar to Masonic practices, Carbonari membership included not only Freemasons but Mafiosi, military officers and politicians. Its initiation ceremony threatened "certain and violent death" for any member who violated the society's secrets. This code of *omertà* was enforced by the Mafiosi in its ranks.

By the 1970s Licio Gelli, the grandmaster of P-2, had developed it into the most powerful political organization in Italy. Important Italian generals, judges and businessmen became members, forming a state within a state which controlled the country. Sindona sponsored Roberto Calvi as a member of P-2, and, from the moment he joined, his rise to the top accelerated, and he became the chairman of the respected Banca Ambrosiana.

Sindona, however, soon overextended himself by purchasing the Franklin National Bank in the United States and buying other companies in Europe, mostly with loans. When a worldwide recession hit because of the OPEC-inspired oil shortage, and interest rates soared, money was made tight, and Sindona's whole empire collapsed. When U.S. auditors moved in to examine his books, they found evidence of fraudulent money transactions, and Sindona was indicted.

With Sindona facing a prison term, Calvi now took his place as the Vatican's chief financial adviser, and for a while he had better luck than his erstwhile mentor. He expanded his own bank by creating foreign branches, with the Vatican bank, IOR, as his partner. A tight-lipped man with reputed "eyes of ice," he now became Italy's most powerful banker, the natural inheritor of all of Sindona's power bases—the Church, the Mafia, and P-2, the secret guild.

But then Calvi reached too far, and the fate that was to end in London began to draw near. He contrived a grand scheme, worthy of his genius, to milk his own bank. Anonymously, he created phantom companies overseas which borrowed money from his bank's foreign branches. Soon hundreds of millions of dollars were lent by the foreign branches to the ghost companies, loans which could never be repaid because the money disappeared. Interestingly, it would be revealed later that the Vatican, under Calvi's guidance, was made a partner in many of these ghost companies, and eventually it had to repay more than $200 million to Banca Ambrosiana's shareholders.

Rumors of the ghost-company swindle filtered through Italy's financial community, but there the all-powerful P-2 protected Roberto Calvi from judicial inquiries—for a price. As a return for this protection, Ambrosiana had to make large and questionable "loans" to P-2 members.

Then, in 1981, disaster struck from an unexpected direction. Investigators looking into Michele Sindona's Mafia connections were led to the address of

Licio Gelli, the P-2 leader, in Rome. In the safe in
Gelli's home police found thirty-two sealed envelopes filled with incriminating documents which recorded bribes by P-2 to judges, politicians and
industrialists. The revelation created one of the greatest scandals in Italian history. The fact that many cabinet members, as well as the head of every branch of
the armed services, were members of this secret
group rocked the nation.

Included in P-2's files was one labeled "Roberto
Calvi," detailing how Gelli had manipulated judicial
authorities to protect the banker, and it was that lead
which eventually climaxed in the unmasking of Calvi's ghost-company swindle. In May 1981 Calvi was
indicted for embezzling tens of millions of dollars,
which had subsequently disappeared. Eventually the
total would be established at no less than $400 mil-
lion, and the Vatican's share amounted to only half.
Where was the rest of the money?

Calvi was arrested and held without bail, but he
shocked his interrogators by claiming innocence. The
swindle hadn't been his creation at all; instead he had
been used by someone else as a front for the scheme.
He was just a tool, he said, for the people who were
really behind the fraud. But he was too frightened to
reveal the identity of those people.

All Italy seethed with speculation. Was it the Sicilian Mafia that controlled Calvi's bank all along, or the
sinister P-2? Or, a question usually asked in hushed
tones, was it certain parties in the Holy See who had
defrauded not only the bank but the Vatican itself?

Calvi stayed mum about his knowledge of the secret
powers behind him, but events were closing in on
him, and one night in prison he apparently attempted
suicide. His lawyer reported that Calvi had taken an

overdose of barbiturates and cut his wrists in his cell, but, as always in Calvi's life, there was controversy. The prison director swore that the suicide attempt had been a fake intended to evoke sympathy, and that Calvi's wrists hadn't been slashed.

On July 20, 1981, Roberto Calvi was found guilty of illegally exporting millions of dollars to his ghost companies, and was sentenced to four years in prison and a $10-million fine. Then he was released on bail, pending his appeal against conviction.

2

Roberto Calvi obviously feared for his life. On June 10, 1982, he jumped bail and fled from Italy. Using a false passport, he flew to Trieste in the private plane of Flavio Carboni, a wheeler-dealer with reputed Mafia connections, who brought along Silvano Vittor, a small-time smuggler, ostensibly to act as a bodyguard for Calvi. Arriving in London after intermediate stops both in Trieste and in Austria, Calvi checked into the Chelsea Cloisters, a hotel tenanted mostly by students, a far drop from the luxury hotels that Calvi had been used to throughout his career as an eminent banker. Carboni, meanwhile, arrived at Heathrow Airport with two beautiful young Austrian girls, Manuela and Michaela Kleinszig, the first said to be his mistress, the other Vittor's girlfriend. All three registered in the classier Hilton Hotel, while Vittor roomed with Calvi in Chelsea.

Carboni claims that he saw Calvi on their first night in London, and that Calvi complained only about his hotel room, which he thought was too small. But later that night, in telephone calls to his daughter and his wife, Calvi expressed only one real concern, fear for his life and the lives of his family. He ordered his daughter to fly at once to her brother's house in Washington, where his wife had already fled and where she would be protected. To his wife he expressed an even more ominous worry: "I don't trust the people I'm with anymore."

On the night of June 17, according to Flavio Carboni's later testimony, he arrived at the Chelsea Cloisters and called Calvi's room. He wanted Calvi to join him and the Kleinszig sisters for dinner. Vittor, the bodyguard, in his testimony, said that Calvi did not want to join the others for dinner, so he went along instead.

It was 11 P.M. when Vittor left Calvi's room, which, as it developed, was the last time he saw Calvi alive. He said that he met Carboni in the lobby and the two men went to a restaurant where the apparently ever lively Kleinszig sisters were waiting. Later Carboni went off with the girls to move from the Hilton to the Sheraton Hotel near Heathrow Airport, while Vittor returned to Calvi's room at 1:30 A.M. He claimed that he found the room empty, and the banker gone. When Calvi didn't return, Vittor said he spent a sleepless night, fearful for his own life, then fled the next morning to Austria. Meanwhile Carboni, alerted by Vittor, also fled, but by a circuitous (and later controversial) route. He flew to Edinburgh for a day, then, using a private plane owned by a "friend," jetted to Switzerland, where he went into hiding.

So the two men who had brought Calvi to London disappeared at once, one with an immediate side trip to Edinburgh that aroused suspicion. In the worldwide tumult after Calvi's body was found, both Carboni and Vittor were eventually tracked down and questioned. They claimed complete innocence, and said they had disappeared only because they had helped Calvi and were now afraid for their own lives.

But, of course, the two men were prime suspects if murder had indeed been done. Not only did they have underworld connections, but Carboni, during the last week of Calvi's life, had made trips to cities all over Europe. Was it in connection with secret bank accounts in which the missing hundreds of millions of dollars were stashed? Had Carboni and his associates decided to grab all the money by killing Calvi?

Carboni and Vittor were not the only suspects. Ominously, it was noted that Roberto Calvi's briefcase had disappeared. According to his wife, this briefcase was "always at his side." The press asked the question, Were there secret documents in that briefcase that the sinister P-2 or the Mafia, or even the Vatican, did not want to be revealed? Did someone in these organizations feel Calvi was about to crack and silence him before he did so?

Few in the press in both England and Italy seemed to doubt that the death was the result of murder, even though the hanging appeared to be a suicide. Reporters went to the scene, and told their readers that an iron ladder from the embankment parapet along the road stood about two feet to the left of the scaffolding of thin pipes. To commit suicide, the paunchy sixtyish banker would have had to climb over the parapet, clamber down the ladder in the night, "acrobatically" swing over to the scaffolding, make his perilous way along slippery iron rungs to its far edge above the river, then tie a rope around the scaffolding and his throat. All this with heavy stones in his pockets and a brick in the front of his trousers.

Further, they asked, why did Calvi walk *four miles* to Blackfriars Bridge to commit suicide in the first place? Why not jump out of a window right at the hotel, or take sleeping pills, if he wanted to die? A long trip to the bridge was not the action a suicidal man would take. In fact, there were bridges closer to his hotel if for some reason he wanted to hang himself before the world. But such a suicide was completely out of character, anyway, for the reclusive banker who had always avoided public exposure in any form.

But what fascinated reporters most of all in this bizarre death was the P-2 connection. Stones on the body, feet under water, the name of the bridge, Blackfriars, were all said to be integral parts of the Masonic ritual associated with P-2. Witchcraft on the Thames!

Surprisingly to the press, however, the police apparently had other ideas about Calvi's death. It wasn't a murder at all, they said. At a stormy press conference at the Snow Hill police station, Commander Hugh Moore, the officer in charge of the Calvi case, announced, "There are no indications at this stage that it was not suicide." In the zeal of the press to find bizarre trails and characters in a murder, Moore said, reporters were ignoring all the facts that supported a theory of suicide. For one thing, if ever there was a night that Calvi would have chosen to commit suicide, it was June 17, 1982. Already on the run, hunted by police, his career in disgrace, Calvi had the following news to absorb that very day:

At a meeting in Milan, the board of Banca Ambrosiana had stripped him of his powers as chairman, and the management of the bank had been transferred to the Bank of Italy, in effect ending Ambrosiana's career as one of Italy's leading banks.

Worse, Graziella Corrocher, Calvi's secretary for

many years, had jumped out of an office window in
Milan that same day, leaving a suicide note which
included the words: "[Calvi] should be twice damned
for the damage he did to the group, and to all of us,
who were at one time so proud of it."

Meanwhile a quiet man in a coroner's office tried to
find the answer to it all. Professor Keith Simpson, the
most respected forensic pathologist in England, and
of great reputation throughout the world, prepared to
perform the autopsy on Roberto Calvi.

He began by looking for telltale bruises on Calvi's
body which would signify violence, and for needle
marks which would reveal the injection of drugs, both
indications of murder. Then he examined the neck
closely to determine whether Calvi had really hanged
himself, or whether he had been strangled beforehand, then strung up on the scaffold to make his death
appear a suicide.

Later Simpson issued his official autopsy report,
which described his findings. These were, in part:

> Deep impression of a noose around the neck and upper
> thyroid level in front and on the left side, rising to a
> suspension point behind the right ear, a single ropeline
> weave pattern, with "asphyxia petechiae" above this
> level, and internally in the heart and lungs . . . No other
> injury to arouse suspicion. No injection marks on the
> body . . . No head injury, or bruising. . . .

A murder by strangling, as forensic scientists know,
almost always produces an impression of the rope in
a complete circle around the neck. Deliberate suspension (suicide by hanging), on the other hand, leaves
an impression of a rope most deeply in the front of the
throat ("upper thyroid level") and also leaves the

mark of the knot. In this autopsy report, that mark is called the "suspension point beyond the right ear." On the basis of his autopsy, Simpson concluded that the impressions he found on Calvi's throat were "those of deliberate suspension and give no cause for suspicion of foul play."

3

Her Majesty's Coroner for London, Dr. David Paul, is an old friend from various international forensic conventions we attend. He's a tall, urbane man with a quick intelligence and a vivid style of speech. The latter talent caused him some trouble at the inquest he conducted into the death of Robert Calvi. In England, unlike America, coroners are part of the judiciary and preside at hearings to determine the cause of death.

More than forty witnesses were heard at that inquest, ranging from police constables and detectives to Odette Morris, a young woman who had accompanied Flavio Carboni on the trip to Edinburgh immediately after Calvi's death. Carboni and Silvano Vittor testified through depositions at the inquest, which was eagerly attended by reporters hoping to hear testimony about Calvi's connections with P-2, the Vatican or the Mafia.

But the most important witness at the inquest was from none of these groups; instead he was Dr. Simpson, who, to the disappointment of the press, confirmed his autopsy findings which had showed that Calvi had not been murdered. The evidence of the rope mark around his neck, and the absence of bruises elsewhere on the body, he said, precluded either an earlier strangling or external violence of any kind.

The other witnesses added nothing about P-2 or the Mafia. Odette Morris indicated that the trip to Edinburgh was just a lark. Police believed that Edinburgh was an unlikely place to go for such a lark, but had no evidence to refute her. The testimony of all of the witnesses did not end until after 7 P.M. Then, after an adjournment, Dr. Paul made his summation.

Paul agreed that it might have been awkward for Calvi to hang himself from that scaffold, but said it would have been equally difficult to *murder* him there. How, Paul asked, could a man of Calvi's weight have been carried down that ladder, then across the gap to the scaffolding, then hanged, without "sustaining some marks upon his body of that carriage across that rather awkward scaffolding?"

As for the possibility that Calvi might have been brought to the bridge by boat, Paul noted that the Thames River current was swift at that point, and asked, "Could a boat be handled with sufficient skill so that it could maintain its position beneath the scaffolding while a heavy man such as Mr. Calvi was supported upright and then suspended from a rope . . . ?"

Finally, Paul explained to the members of the jury the three verdicts they could reach: suicide, murder or an open verdict. And it was here that his vivid phrase-making created trouble. "The open verdict may seem like a super open door to scuttle through if you are in any difficulty about returning another verdict," he said. "Let me tell you that this was not, never has been, and I hope will never be a convenient, comfortable way out."

At ten o'clock that same night, the jury foreman

stood up in the small coroner's court and announced, "By a majority verdict the jury has decided that the deceased killed himself."

In Italy, the verdict was greeted with derision in the press, but a more concrete challenge emerged from Roberto Calvi's family. Because three million dollars in insurance money was involved, they appealed the suicide verdict, citing Dr. Paul's remarks in his summation, which seemed to steer the jury away from an open verdict. They also claimed that the extraordinary length of the inquest meant the jury was no doubt fatigued and that that too had influenced the verdict.

On March 29, 1983, the appeal was granted, a very rare occurrence, and the public prepared for a second round in the fascinating Calvi affair at a new inquest. Dr. Arthur Gordon Davies, the coroner from Southwark, acted as judge at the new hearing. And this time, when Dr. Simpson took the stand, he was severely challenged. In fact, George Carman, the Calvi family's new attorney, managed to get Simpson to agree that it would indeed have been easier for men in a boat to kill Calvi than for Calvi to hang himself from the scaffold. Carman then suggested a reason for the absence of bruises. Certain drugs like ethyl chloride, which does not leave traces, might have been used to immobilize Calvi. If no injection marks had been found, that might have been because Calvi was injected in hard-to-detect areas, such as under the hair on his head. Simpson thought that speculation was farfetched, but admitted that it was, of course, possible.

During the inquest, Carman made certain the jury knew all about Carboni's Mafia connections and the mysterious peregrinations of Carboni, Vittor and the

Kleinszig sisters, who had checked in and out of various hotels and made unexplained trips to different cities all over Europe before and after Calvi's death. For example, Carman asked Michaela Kleinszig, "Was it an *ordinary* week for you—as the mother of a child—to go to Switzerland, Amsterdam and London in three days?"

The proceedings came to a close, and on June 27, 1983, the jury foreman announced the jury's decision: "We find an open verdict, sir."

And with those words the mysterious death of a banker hanging under a London bridge in broad daylight was officially declared "unsolved."

4

In August 1984 I was in Oxford, England, to attend the International Forensic Sciences conference, and while there I arranged to interview Dr. Paul in the Coroner's office to discuss the Calvi case. The interview proved surprising and revealing.

In the first inquest Paul had seemed to deride the idea of an open verdict. Now, two years later, he said, "I think the open verdict was the *right* verdict. There was too much evidence on both sides to justify anything else." His remarks about an open verdict which had caused so much controversy meant only that such a finding would always be "uncomfortable" for a jury, because it would leave the death unsolved.

Then he told me some fascinating details about Calvi's death which I had never seen published. "His shoes were muddy," Paul said. "If he committed suicide, how did his shoes get muddy when he allegedly stepped off a city street and onto a ladder to hang himself? Further, and even more important, his suit was wet up to the armpits. If you're going to hang yourself you don't jump into deep water up to your shoulders."

Paul believes he has the answer to both mysteries. Calvi had walked along the foreshore of the river when the tide was low. The water there, Paul said, is very dark and looks deeper than it is. In fact, he said, during his investigation of the scene the next day, one of his policemen had dropped his electronic pager into the water. "A frogman jumped in to retrieve it and almost broke his legs. The water was only knee-high."

Paul thinks that Calvi, in a suicidal despair, was walking along the shore of the Thames that night, and that that was where he made his shoes muddy. Believing the water was deep, he placed stones in his pockets and jumped into the Thames to drown himself, causing his suit to be wet up to the armpits. When he failed to drown because the water was shallow, he kept walking along the shore, eventually arriving at Blackfriars Bridge. There he saw an orange nylon rope dangling from a scaffold and conceived his idea of suicide by hanging. Paul said boatmen always keep such ropes there, and at other points on the Thames, for use if they need to tie up. Calvi hanged himself with the rope, leaving a damp suit and muddy shoes as clues to a previous attempt at suicide by drowning.

"That's my theory," Paul said, "but only if the tide was low at the time. You see, the great trouble in this case is that we don't know *when* Calvi died, so we don't know if the tide was high or low. The body temperature, which usually gives us our main clue, was worthless in this case because, one way or another, the body had been immersed in water during the night."

I asked Paul about the fact that Calvi would have needed the skills of an acrobat to commit suicide on that scaffolding. He replied, "People make a lot of the fact that it would have been difficult for Calvi to hang himself from that scaffolding. But it wouldn't have been *extraordinarily* difficult. Two feet isn't that wide a distance between the ladder and the scaffold. So it wasn't quite as 'acrobatic' as the Calvi family's lawyer kept implying."

But why, I asked Paul, if he personally seemed to lean toward suicide, did he approve an open verdict? "Well, for one thing," he said, "there's Calvi's mustache."

This sounded so much like Sherlock Holmes that I smiled, and Paul smiled, too. "Yes, I know, the dog that didn't bark. In this case, it's identical. This was the mustache that wasn't there. Calvi shaved it off the day before the murder. To me, that is evidence of a man who is trying to change his appearance because he's afraid of violence from someone and therefore is trying to hide his identity, not a man who is about to commit suicide. In fact, the night before he died he wouldn't enter the Hilton Hotel, because he was afraid he would be recognized. He was definitely frightened for his life."

Then, Paul added, the "obvious" questions also bothered him. Why walk all the way to Blackfriars Bridge, four miles from his hotel, to commit suicide? Why not jump out of a window at the hotel instead? "We checked the drugs in his room. Of all the medications he had, none would have killed him, so that explains why he didn't commit suicide with sleeping pills. But he didn't have to walk four miles to kill himself, either.

"In the final analysis, I don't think he had any *pre-meditated* idea of committing suicide, if, indeed, he did so," Paul said. "I believe that as he walked along the shore of the river the idea came to him, and he acted on impulse and, no doubt, despair."

Then he added, "Incidentally, the Italian police have acted rather oddly on this case. I understand a Scotland Yard detective went to Italy twice to interrogate Flavio Carboni, the key witness and chief suspect, and never was allowed to do so. And, equally strange, I also hear that the Italian authorities never released the *complete* contents of the suicide note that Calvi's secretary left behind. Are there still secrets of the Calvi affair the Italian authorities are hiding? I don't know."

I thanked Dr. Paul and joked with him about the white wig on a shelf behind his desk. As part of the judiciary, coroners in England wear a wig and a robe at their inquests. I tried on the wig, and the sight would have frightened many Los Angeles bureaucrats —as well as my friends.

But the next day, after my interview with Dr. Paul, my mind still dwelt on this most baffling forensic case. Above all, my mind fastened on the information that when Calvi's body was found his suit was wet up to the armpits.

I researched the tides of the Thames on the night of June 17–18, 1982. High tide registered at 21.8 feet and occurred at 2:58 A.M. Low tide was six hours later, at 8:30 A.M. At 7:30 A.M., Calvi had been found with his feet dangling under water.

Calvi had last been seen in his hotel at 11:30 P.M.,

and had disappeared by one, which meant that, unless he delayed his suicide until dawn, the river was "up." Therefore, Dr. Paul's theory that Calvi had got his suit wet in an attempt to drown himself at low tide would be tenable only if he did this at daybreak, which would have been an unlikely time for suicide, with Londoners going to work. I believe it was far more likely that the suicide—or murder—had been committed in the middle of the dark night. If so, the Thames was at high tide. And I wonder if that fact might be the long-unfound key to the mystery of Calvi's bizarre death.

In both inquests, it had been said that the hanging of Calvi by murderers would have been difficult. Carrying his body from a ladder to a scaffold to hang him seemed too awkward and cumbersome to be imagined, and lifting his body from a boat seemed almost equally as difficult.

But not at high tide. Calvi could have been brought to the scaffolding in a boat when the tide was at its crest. With the boat riding near the top of the scaffolding, it would have been simple to attach his body to the pipes, and to place stones in his pockets to make certain that, when he died, he dangled vertically under water, and therefore wouldn't be seen until the boat with its murderers had cleared the scene and the tide went down. Finally, his shoes had gotten muddy when he was transferred from the shore into the boat.

That is my theory. And I only wish London's two greatest detectives, Sherlock Holmes and Hercule Poirot, were real and alive to solve this extraordinary death which seems to resist explanation either as a murder or as a suicide.

Was it witchcraft on the Thames? One doubts the theory as being too fantastic, but my own belief in the high-tide factor as a possible clue caused me to be somewhat chilled when I was told that part of the secret P-2 ritual oath includes the threat of death for traitors in "the ebb and flow of the tides."

Afterword

Although my career as Chief Medical Examiner of Los Angeles County was abruptly terminated and I now work at Los Angeles County General Hospital as a pathologist and teacher, I no longer feel that I am in exile. I have made many new friends, I like my work, and I enjoy my relationships with my professional colleagues. Indeed, I am fortunate to be part of a lively institution devoted to the healing arts.

But my main passion is, and always will be, forensic science, that misunderstood, almost hidden field of medicine which seems to emerge into the light of public awareness only when one or another medical examiner, in one or another city, is fired.

Recently, I received a telephone call from my friend Bill Eckert, the forensic pathologist whose organization, INFORM, in Wichita, Kansas, serves as a central clearinghouse and historical library for forensic scientists around the world. "Isn't it something?" he said. "It seems that sooner or later every coroner finds himself in terrible trouble."

Why is that? I asked myself after his call. Are the physicians who hold jobs as medical examiners deficient in skills? I doubt it. Are they *all* bad managers? I doubt that too. I believe the explanation arises from two deeper sources: a lack of understanding of the mission of the medical examiner's office, and, worse, an unspoken fear of anything associated with death. The mere rumor of wrongful practices in a department which deals with the dead strikes a raw nerve.

The fact is that medical examiners are torn and buffeted by pressure groups on every side. The law wants evidence to find and convict murderers; defendants demand evidence to prove their innocence. Families of victims of alleged police brutality seek justice, as do the police officers accused of the crimes. Relatives with estates or insurance money at stake desire judgments that will aid their cases. Friends of the deceased want reputations kept whole by suppressing evidence. And other pressures too numerous to detail are present every day.

What guide do we medical examiners have to make our way through these explosive minefields? The principle is simple. You must state the truth bravely, no matter how the evidence bothers, dismays or angers various pressure groups. But that, I know from my own experience, can prove costly. I believe that my dismissal came about as the result of my decision to tell the facts about the role that alcohol played in the deaths of Natalie Wood and William Holden. I do not regret that decision, for today I am more certain than ever that our field of medicine must be dedicated to aiding the living by learning from the dead. It is a conviction I have tried to express in a *haiku*.

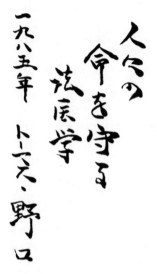

人々の命を守る法医学

一九八五年　トーマス・野口

The real contribution of forensic medicine is to protect and save valuable human lives.

I hope that I have, in the cases reported in this book, made a contribution of my own to the understanding of the mission of forensic science and some of its techniques and methods. And I hope something more: that the book may encourage others to choose our science as their career. If more and more of our brilliant young medical students enter the profession of forensic science, the loss of my own job will turn out to be a blessing, for it gave me the inspiration to write this book.

Meanwhile, I intend to continue my legal battle to regain my office, and to serve my profession as best I know how in all the years of my life.

Acknowledgments

I would like to thank all my forensic colleagues in America and in Europe, who assisted me, directly or indirectly, in the research for this book, and in particular these forensic experts and lawyers:

William Eckert, M.D., Professor Herbert Mac-Donell, Thomas Puccio, J.D., Francis Buck, M.D., Clive Taylor, M.D., Ph.D., Keith P. Inman, Herbert Fisher, J.D., Michael Russakow, J.D., Robert E. Litman, M.D., John Thornton, Doctor of Criminology, U.S.C., Lester Luntz, D.D.S., David Paul, M.D.

My thanks also to my researchers: Valerie Ulam, Janice Roehl, Jacqueline Riley, Karen Emmons, Ann Lakos, Sylvia Kutz, Lori Andiman.

And special gratitude to our editors, Burton Beals and Fred Hills, and to our literary agents, Arthur and Richard Pine.

About the Author:

Thomas Noguchi was born in Japan and came to the United States in 1952 to complete his residency in pathology at Loma Linda University, California. In 1960 he joined the Los Angeles County Coroner's office as Deputy Medical Examiner, and subsequently was appointed Chief Medical Examiner. After he left that post in a storm of controversy, his professional colleagues elected him President of the National Association of Medical Examiners. He is now Vice-President of the World Association on Medical Law.

Joseph DiMona has been called by *The New York Times* "an example of the successful collaborator whose own name may be as recognizable as the subject's." In addition to his collaboration with controversial figures such as H. R. Haldeman *(The Ends of Power)* and Dr. Noguchi *(Coroner)*, he has written best-selling novels including *Last Man at Arlington* and *To the Eagle's Nest*. Mr. DiMona is a lawyer and member of the bar of the District of Columbia.